KERYGMA AND DOGMA

MYSTERIUM SALUTIS

Edited by

JOHANNES FEINER
MAGNUS LÖHRER
THOMAS F. O'MEARA

KERYGMA AND DOGMA

KARL RAHNER
AND KARL LEHMANN

WITHDRAWN

HERDER AND HERDER

1969
HERDER AND HERDER NEW YORK
232 Madison Avenue, New York, N.Y. 10016

Original Edition: *Mysterium Salutis*, volume 1, Einsiedeln, 1965, pp. 622-703. Edited by Thomas F. O'Meara, and translated by William Glen-Doepel.

Nihil obstat: Leo J. Steady, Censor Librorum
Imprimatur: ✠ Robert F. Joyce, Bishop of Burlington
October 19, 1968

Library of Congress Catalog Card Number: 68-55090
© 1969 by Herder and Herder, Inc.
Manufactured in the United States

CONTENTS

FOREWORD

With this somewhat traditional and Hellenic title, joining *kerygma* to *dogma*, Karl Rahner and his theological associate, Karl Lehmann, offer contemporary light on two of the most difficult and widespread theological paradoxes facing contemporary Christian theology. Their combined work builds upon Father Rahner's other works on the nature and task of theology, the evolution of dogma, tradition and revelation, the New Testament and its theologies, faith and the teaching office of the Church. Father Lehmann is competent in both philosophy (specializing in the mutually-influencing dialogue between Martin Heidegger and Christian thought) and theology. Both at Munich and at Münster, he has served as the unofficial director of resource and service people working with Father Rahner. Often responsible for the research and completion of some aspects of the varied projects of the German Jesuit, he has recently in this and certain other works become his co-worker.

At the bottom of the reflections of this book (which generously includes extensive histories and documentation of the ideas of early Christian kerygma and historical formulation and evolution of dogma), there are actually two problems. (1) Now that we have recognized the complex character of the origins of each New Testament writing, and have admitted the need for a scholarly and many-leveled historical criticism in finding and understanding the "message" of the New Testament, now that we have introduced "theology" into the very

7

chapters of John, Luke, Paul, and so forth, how will we find "what" the New Testament is talking about? Is there a message, gospel, doctrine, that is, kerygma? (2) How can there be anything like dogma (which includes by definition the permanent, the lasting, the canonized in language), when historicity and linguistics have shown all language to be, despite any claim of the divine, quite human and always historical?

Both of these problems are of the utmost importance to Christians today. They are not the concern of "scholars" but influence the pastoral ministry and every level of religious education. They are central to the recent Council, recent encyclicals, the wrestling and polarization about the ideas and structures for renewing the Roman Catholic Church. The origins of the ambiguous nature of kerygma and dogma often lie with Protestant theological scholarship, and the same problems are present for these Churches. Many believe that modern theological scholarship is undermining Protestant Church life. Is the increasing appeal of fundamentalist sects a phenomenon which is related to the growing difficulty of a practical understanding of how *sola scriptura* is still possible? Rudolf Bultmann claims to have carried his particular version of dialectical theology—Lutheran justification by faith—beyond the dimension of action and will into the intellectual sphere. Faith has no object of God's self-disclosure, no revelatory events in a real salvation history. Every objectified revelation is theology (or mythology), the clothing of God's acceptance of men in things and persons and stories and "history" which have only one purpose—the disclosure in faith of my acceptance by God. Hence, to speak of God is ultimately to speak of man; revelation is the affirmation of the reality of positive existence. But if Bultmann has exalted this principle of the Reformation, he has with his biblical criticism raised to an almost world-wide level the problem of whether the Scriptures are talking about

8

anything, communicating anything. Can the Scriptures claim to be involved, not only in existential and personal religious history, but in a secular history which has at points become also a saving history, be taken seriously?

Kerygma and Dogma, while considering the varied questions of this two-fold topic, seems to indicate that there is a basic problem for both. How can the definitive, the incarnate, the divine, the revelatory, the prophetic be present in the human, either at its beginnings or in its development? Jesus of Nazareth is a human teacher with methods aimed at a certain audience, culture, and time. And then, his thought comes to us—our immediate verbal witness being the New Testament —through words which never claimed to be a reporter's transcription. From the beginning, the varied kinds of thought forms—parables, modes of discourse, Semitic and Hellenic interpretations, religious nuances—are present. What is a kerygma? Is there one, and how do we find it and verify our discovery, or better, our laying bare, our disclosure? Who preached what?

The second problem, that of dogma, is allied to this. Granted that the New Testament is a privileged record, a privileged "theology," can we place any confidence, especially if the kerygma is so influenced by man and history, in dogma? Dogmas are even weaker in permanence than the privileged interpretations of the New Testament. The dogmatic often seems to be the enemy of the Christian; yet Christ's work does imply truth and permanence.

It is difficult even to phrase these questions adequately. Neither Rahner nor Lehmann would claim to have fully answered these burning theological questions. The importance of the work is its offering of a scholarly and Catholic introduction, in its respect for continuity and its expectation of the possibility of the presence of the Spirit in the history of the Church's

9

reflection. Because they face the two-fold problem outlined above—a problem made increasingly thorny through more and more conflicts over Church renewal in the Christian communities (as opposed to joint planning sessions)—, because they are willing to ask the question in its difficult form—How can we let the real, lasting, revealed message disclose itself from out of its historical garb?—their ideas deserve not only to be read but to be reflected upon.

THOMAS F. O'MEARA, O.P.

10

KERYGMA AND DOGMA

INTRODUCTION

In this work we will distinguish the statements of dogma not only from kerygma—from proclamation, and from preaching in the strict theological sense of the word—but also from statements of a non-religious character (even those concerning religious matters, if such are possible), so that in the end we will have a clear idea of what is common to dogma and also to kerygma in terms of strict theological statement.

It will also be necessary for us to distinguish kerygmatic statements, as defined in the narrowest sense, from scriptural statements properly so called. We must keep in mind the fact that in Scripture revelation is not simply coming into the world, as an event, for the first time. Rather there is within Scripture what we might call not precisely kerygma but, let us say, exemplary theological reflexion. Catholic theology concerning the inspired nature of Scripture can certainly accommodate this form, since inspiration, as is well known, does not preclude the possibility of markedly different literary types within the one word of God.

I. KERYGMA

A. The Linguistic Usage of "Kerygma"

In the apostolic community the homily was never meant to be simply the "repetition" of fixed and rigidly conceived kerygma which would only need to be *applied* in concrete doctrine and pastoral exhortation. The kerygma is certainly, as *apostolic* kerygma, complete and perfect, and as the "fundamental" kerygma it constitutes the criterion of all further kerygmatic utterance; but it is at the same time a continuing and actualizing process and event. Heinz Schürmann rightly points out that "even the post-apostolic proclamation of the Church may rightly call itself kerygma."[1] (See 2 Timothy 4, 2.) The written word alone does not, simply by being there, convey revelation, because Scripture alone, in that sense, is not yet the full measure of revelation, although it does give knowledge of it. In the true and actual history of the Church this kerygma, which comes from the fundamental proclamation of the kingdom of God which took place with Jesus and which takes Jesus as its constant criterion, is able to make this original Gospel concretely present in the world to which it is addressed. Thus revelation does not become actualized until it is proclaimed. Inasmuch as what one calls "tradition" offers the interpretation of the Christ event by the

---

[1] "Kerygma," in *Lexikon für Theologie und Kirche* VI (Freiburg, 1961), p. 124.

15

spiritual authority conferred by the risen Lord, while in the service of Scripture and with its gaze always directed towards it, nonetheless there is already present in kerygma, properly understood, the element of "tradition." It is only in the interplay of the two that the *reality* of what is merely written in Scripture comes to be, that is, can be proclaimed. The testimony to the "fundamental" kerygma is its element of "tradition," already operative in it, insofar as it *is* kerygma. Another mode of paradosis is the witness of the profession of faith (for example, St. Paul in 1 Corinthians 15). But here the question arises of the origin and authority of such faith and proclamation. Within the limits of this work we are naturally unable to go into the reasons why this truly authorized preaching is possible only in the mouth of the Church. Kerygma and the Church belong together in a way which has numerous dimensions.

Nevertheless, there does remain the dilemma of recent Protestant theology, to the effect that on the one hand it is no longer concerned with the origin and legitimacy of the kerygma, but on the other does not desire, nor is able, to pursue further the "demand" or "request" for faith (or at least the demand that one should be *open* to faith) which is contained in the kerygma itself. This dilemma will persist so long as it is formulated in terms of a more or less private search for "contemporaneity" with the historical Jesus or with what is a fairly "abstract" kerygma of Christ, for not only is any guide or "tradition" offering a way into the event or belief refused, but also the history of Christianity and all historical distance is either ignored, consciously denied, or negatively destroyed. The question of "transmission" is not answered and can hardly even be adequately asked. The problems of this position become clearer if they are pursued into the realm of that kerygmatic proclamation which we call the "sacraments." Authority and transmission then raise the question of *office* within the Church.

It should be clear thus far that the word "kerygma" may correctly be used to describe both the act and the contents of the Church's proclamation; the word has no fortuitous definition describing it in minimal terms. Indeed, it is within the range of its more complex sense, embracing or at least potentially indicating the full reality of Christian proclamation, that the word "kerygma" has been and is still used in kerygmatically oriented pastoral theology. Nevertheless, criticism has been appropriately made of the fact that in such theology it is chiefly the purely material character of kerygma which is stressed—the "contents" of "doctrine"—with the consequence that the really important feature of kerygma—the element of actualizing interpretation, of enlightening proclamation and "address" (especially in its ecclesiological sense) —is inadequately presented.

The kerygma, which in the universal breadth of its significance transmits revelation within the framework of the historical Church, has also its own history, one that is not simply identical with a history of dogma, or of spirituality, or so forth. Josef Jungmann and F. X. Arnold, along with their former pupils, have shown us many types of proclamation by the Church. Changes in the "Easter sermon," the place of Christ in prayer and catechetics, the idea of the Church or the communion of saints, and eschatological preaching are but a few examples. But precisely in this area much remains to be done by way of "illuminating the historical development of the kerygma, recognizing and correcting distortions, recovering particular happy solutions of former times and using them to regenerate the present."[2]

[2] F. X. Arnold, "Kerygma und Theologie," in *Katechetisches Wörterbuch* (Freiburg, 1961), p. 396.

Thus kerygma, in its fullest sense, is the actual and historically determined proclamation of the word of God in the Church by a proclaimer, authorized by God, who bears witness. This word, spoken by the proclaimer in the power of the Spirit and in faith, hope, and charity, brings into being and makes present what is proclaimed (the promise of God to man) as an evangelical message of salvation and as a committing and judging power; it does this in such a way, moreover, that salvation history, both beginning and end, becomes present "now" in Jesus Christ, and that this word, which has become an event in what is said and heard, can be received by the listener in faith and love.

With this general summing up of the nature of kerygma we conclude this part of our investigation in order to proceed to a more systematic consideration of the inner structure of kerygma.

B. The Factual Meaning and Modes of Realization of Kerygma

We take up now the question why theological discourse on the modes of realization of the transmission of revelation gave preference to the liturgical word. The answer is that this was justified because the word of God spoken in the liturgy, as its central element, is the word of God in all its fullness of being. For the liturgy, primarily in the celebration of the Eucharist and in the sacraments, is based on the word, effective *ex opere operato*, which is spoken as the *word of God*. In other words, the liturgy actually contains within itself the reality which it states, and truly makes this reality present in the life of the community and in the decisive situations of the individual.

This effective statement and promise does not take place merely because of the transcendence of God, but is at the same time a promise which comes from the historical saving event—anamnesis. Thus it is the tradition of the historical saving event which is stated in the kerygma and at the same time made present. This means that general abstract truths are stated in the kerygma only insofar as they are a necessary part of the saving event or are inevitably stated when the saving event is stated. Since this saving event is still taking place, the one kerygma which still proclaims it is always the "coming of the Lord," the promise of the final revelation of what is stated and made present in it.

Thus all kerygma has, in different degrees according to the particular nature of the kerygma, a "prognostic" character, as do the sacraments. The saving event becomes present in the kerygma in a way related to its origin and future, which come together in the kerygma as a present experience. Kerygma is always anamnesis and prophecy at once. What conditions the authority of the man who proclaims it is the fact that the saving event is indeed being made present through his proclamation (in distinction to the mere communication of a past or general truth which is always and everywhere accessible). The proclaimer must derive the actual, self-authenticating saving event historically from Christ, and be endowed with his authority. With this authority he must be able to act and speak in the name of the whole community of salvation. His kerygma must be based on the reality of salvation within him. Either he must possess, as a man who is justified, this reality of salvation as his own sanctification, or he must at least speak from within the community of the Church, which is always holy, and bear witness to its kerygma.

Because of these elements within it, the word that is spoken in the central acts of the liturgy is simply the word of God

19

in its fullness and most effective power, and therefore represents, in the fullest and most primary sense, what is meant by "kerygma."

However, in order to grasp the full significance of this word we must include, in addition to the elements already mentioned, the idea that the self-communication of the triune God through *grace* is already basically given and effective in the hearer of this word (offered or even accepted), so that the hearing of the kerygma is made possible by the same reality which is proclaimed as present and effective. Only in this way does the kerygma of the Church itself become fully present and real, does it become truly an *event* of salvation, by becoming, as word filled with the proclaimed reality, the salvation of him who hears it.

In addition, there is another aspect which has emerged far more clearly in our own day than in earlier periods of salvation history: hearing belief takes place in the Church.

Here there is another element which has become important, one conditioned by the ecclesiological quality of kerygma. In contrast to earlier periods of salvation history it is primarily the salvation community *as a whole* which serves as the foundation of the religious service of the individual community and which is expressed in it. Since listening faith is *always* given in *this* Church because of the eschatological character of the salvation history of the New Testament as is seen both historically and socially *as* given, the kerygma has not only the character of the word of God to men, but also necessarily at the same time the character of a testimony of belief—that is, of the word of man to God. This testimony must be seen not only as a confession of faith which commits one to the Church, but primarily as the praise of God himself, whereby in adoration salvation is celebrated and declared to be an event of the free grace and fidelity of God. The kerygma has neces-

20

sarily a doxological character: it is a word from and to God.

The fact that this kerygmatic word of the liturgy has its highest realization as a saving event in the celebration of the Lord's Supper—that is, that it takes place through the community, in it, and for it (which is, in turn, founded in the covenant character of the salvation of Christ in his Church, which proclaims itself in the Eucharist as the new and eternal covenant)—implies the publication of the kerygma. Thus it follows that the general validity of the Church's kerygma, and hence its dogma, does not depend merely on the objective truth of the statement, after the manner of a metaphysical proposition, but has from the start a dynamic universality directed towards the creation of the salvation community. It is not a question of a truth which has all the time been open to discovery, but of the truth of a God who reveals himself in personal love out of his absolute transcendence, that is, of a truth which exists for all men because God, in his freely given love, desires to reveal himself to all men. This personal self-revelation of God, which makes his truth, in itself existing only for him, into our truth, takes place not only in the private inner world of the individual—that dimension in which everyone is unique and cannot be represented by anyone else, and which has historical manifestation; it takes place also in actual salvation history and has on that account a truly public character.

Thus the kerygma has basically and from the beginning a social character; it is the statement of the truth of the community as such. As a saving event it is naturally directed towards that innermost center of man in which he opens himself in his inalienable freedom to the God of grace by the strength of grace. But the social and public character of the kerygma contains also the possibility of an ambiguous and distorted appearance in the public world. This is the reason for the existence of misunderstandings, misinterpretations, and superstition surrounding religion, and for their power. Faith appears as obscurantism; the miracle of belief as a "miracle" on show. Faith *qua* faith stands in this double light as long as its public and social effect is under view. This fact emerges even more clearly from an analysis of the Gospel of the evangelists: the kerygma involves the possibility that, to put it quite simply, the proclamation may be correct and yet faith may be wrong or bad.

In spite of all the mutal interdependence between publicness and true personal decision in the heart of the individual (without that meaning an escape into false inwardness), the difference and the tension between these two areas emerge in the kerygma. Sacramental theology distinguishes between a valid and a "fruitful" sacrament. The realized salvation of the individual is not an immediately tangible fact in the sphere of the immediate history and socialness of the Church—which does not, after all, anticipate the judgement of God. Accordingly, we must distinguish in the kerygma between the valid kerygma and what in an individual case is in fact effective. But even as "only" valid the kerygma is in its nature the call to a decision which brings salvation or damnation. The proclamation of the good news is filled with an inner dynamism and has a degree of effectiveness which even the strongest opposition of the most unwilling hearer cannot completely destroy; it opens up reality. The New Testament interpretation of the "proclamation" which we have outlined above possesses, according to Protestant exegetes as well, a certain "independence" precisely through the power of its presence. But precisely as a kerygma which is valid in this way, it does not seek to be merely valid, but of its very nature to bring about a real decision in a man in favor of the salvation which is contained in the proclamation, and thus to be fruitful. Hence

22

the kerygma has at all times and in all places, even in those perversions of its publicness (ridicule, jokes, contempt, but also false triumphalism, magic cults, and so forth), the character of a call to decision.

As we have already said, the kerygma has its fullest reality in the celebration of the Eucharist, because it is here that all of its elements reach their most original and highest form. Obviously, this eucharistic kerygma cannot be reduced to what sacramental theology calls the word-form of the sacramental, which is absolutely essential for the effective making-present of the body and blood of the Lord. The Eucharist is the "celebration" of the community, and the sacrament must not only be validly performed, but also accepted in justifying faith. All of the verbal elements of this celebration, which are necessary according to the given circumstances in order to ensure a eucharistic celebration in faith, share in an essential way in the kerygma—which not only takes place on the *occasion* of the Eucharist, but is what the celebration *is*. The way in which this kerygma takes place in detail varies according to time and circumstances. It can be the reading of the Scripture, the prayer of the community, the homily, parenesis paranesis, and so on. All of these are possible as forms of one and the same kerygma which takes place in this celebration. If we desire to distinguish these various modes and forms from the sacramental words (in the technical sense current in theology today), in spite of the fact that they are an essential part of a concrete celebration of the Eucharist in faith—an undertaking which is justified by their greater variability as against the form of the sacrament—then with all their differences they may be grouped together under the one idea of "mystagogy," by which we mean both the introduction to the participation in faith in the eucharistic celebration and the participation itself by the individual in the celebration.

23

If we are allowed this use of the word, which seems indicated by the unifying factor in the various modes and forms discussed, then we may say that mystagogy in the celebration of the Eucharist is the most original and fullest type of kerygma (after the sacramental word, in the narrowest sense). This mystagogy is given also, but not solely, in what is commonly called mystagogic preaching.

Around this mystagogy, that is, around the liturgical kerygma, there are grouped, derived from it, the "homily" and "catechesis." These forms derive from kerygma because —in respect of the degree of authorization, intention, and possibility of making present the saving event in its "sacramental" sign and in its faithful acceptance, and in respect of their character as a call to the community, as a call to decision—they prepare for it or bring it to its full effect, while never of themselves reaching the full reality of the kerygma. Nonetheless, these kerygmatic derivatives are unavoidably necessary within the plurality of human dimensions and for man's self-realization, and they are found too from the very beginning of the Church's life. Their only condition is that they actually have as their object what is proclaimed and made present in the actual kerygma. The kerygma's expressible content is the Christ event in salvation history, his death and resurrection and all that is implied therein, and this content is expressible even when the statement of homily or catechesis does not seek to be, in the full sense, kerygma or mystagogy. This is already seen simply in the fact that Scripture, even when it is not made present for the assembled community in the authorized word of the kerygma and is accepted in the faith of the hearer, is still regarded by the Church as the word of God even though at this level it can be nothing but "doctrinal writing." But, of course, all of these derivative forms of the kerygma have meaning and justification only if

24

they do not forget their origin in the actual kerygma, and lead back to it.

The distinct idea and necessity of what is called the dogmatic teaching of the Church or "dogma" are to be understood from the nature of dogma.

II. DOGMA

A. The Etymological History and Development of the Meaning of "Dogma"

If we seek to distinguish between "kerygma" and "dogma" and see how they are related, then after clarifying the nature of kerygma we shall have to proceed to throw some light upon the idea of "dogma," especially as it has been somewhat out of favor. "Dogma" suggests the idea of a rigid doctrinal system, of constraint of conscience, of high-sounding statements containing venerable ideas which have nonetheless become so far-removed from the original Gospel that they appear to conceal belief rather than reveal it. The appeal to dogma is for many nothing other than the conjuring of sancrosanct formulas the endless explanations of which prove a hindrance to faith itself. Further, any apriorily prescribed formal authority or obedient submission to traditional statements can no longer be asked of anyone in the modern world, because it is part of the dignity of enlightened man to submit only to what his own intellect has critically examined and then is able to experience and acknowledge as meaningful and "acceptable."

Naturally, it is not possible for us to go now into all of the problems relating to the idea of dogma. That would mean pursuing the whole course of modern thinking, particularly as regards the concepts of "autonomy," "reason," and so forth, right down to the most recent questions of a uni-

27

versal hermeneutics which—not unrelated to the general trend of modern intellectual history—is once again and now more positively concerned with what might be called the justification of the dogmatic mode of thinking. Here we can only go into the correct meaning of the *traditional* idea of dogma. And even though we shall endeavor to avoid over-simplification and over-narrow interpretation, this will not really be enough, for only a more thorough investigation would clarify the structure of a truth which a community professes to believe. We would also have to take into account such associated questions as finding, preserving, and transmitting this truth. Such a comprehensive and difficult task still remains to be done. Here we will see whether and how much an investigation into the history of the idea of dogma is of value towards defining it.

1. THE IDEA OF DOGMA IN MEDIEVAL THEOLOGY

With all of the variations which develop in the fourth and fifth centuries in the use of the word "dogma," one cannot still maintain, as it is often attempted, that the idea of "dogma" finds its final form in the medieval era and is generally used in subsequent ages in this unchanging sense. Actually, in subsequent centuries "dogma" is used as a generic idea: "*dogmata patrum*" are merely passages out of, for example, Augustine and Ambrose; "*dogmata fidei*," "*dogmata Christi*," are contrasted with the "*pestifera et mortifera dogmata*" (see *Summa Theologiae*, II-II, q. 11, a. 2, "Sed contra"). In any case, the medieval theologians of high scholasticism do not use the word "dogma" very often, not even St. Thomas. Thus the actual history of the word is not of much help here, for medieval theology uses in a far more fundamental sense the word *"articulus"* when it wants to refer to what we today generally call "dogma."

What is notable when we compare the medieval idea of "dogma" with our usage today (and especially the vulgar pejorative application) is the difference in perspective. Dogma is not primarily a binding formula taken over from an external authority which it is incumbent as a duty on the consciences of men to believe. The idea does not have primarily this juridical quality, this appeal to a formal authority and the obedience demanded by it. "Dogma," for St. Thomas, is not determined by the "objective" boundaries of a pure *"fides divina"* and qualified by the question of the theological *degree of certainty*, rather is its correspondence with belief equally part of the doctrinal character of dogma. The significance of what is to be believed is an important element of dogma, and this conception of dogma as ordered towards eternal life and as the beginning of the possibility of eternal happiness itself so clarifies inner faith, filled with vital strength and tending towards the same eternal life and happiness, that many objections which are generally raised against such ideas as "dogma" become almost pointless.

Accordingly, further investigation would probably show that the change in meaning in the history of the word "dogma" and its equivalents runs almost parallel with the use of the ideas *"fides"* and *"haeresis,"* which A. Lang has pursued. High scholasticism evinces no notable interest of a theoretical kind in merely objective certainty of faith, in the light of which *"fides divina"* and *"veritates mediate revelatae"* are later distinguished from one another. High scholasticism distinguishes between *"articuli fidei"* and derived propositions according to the principle of the significance of the contents, not according

29

to a dogmatic ground for certainty. *"Fides"* and *"haeresis"* are used in a more comprehensive sense, in which is included what is called only *"fides indirecta"* or *"credibilia secundaria."* The quality of a *"veritas fidei"* we ascribe today only to those truths which are vouched for in divine revelation. The criterion is whether they belong to formal revelation, the objective area of *"fides divina."* Medieval theology, at least up to the Council of Trent, measured the area of "belief" by the extent of the inner commitment to a total moral and religious claim. "Theologians sought to establish, not what claims can be made for *'fides divina'* according to dogmatic epistemology, but what from a practical religious attitude must be placed within the responsibility of Christian faith and the jurisdiction of the Church's doctrinal discipline."[1]

A genuine and living faith cannot be limited to those truths which are directly revealed, but embraces everything that belongs in any way to those truths, whether as a basis and a precondition, as a consequence and an effect, and so forth. The important thing in faith is the moral and religious attitude of *obedience* in faith, whereas in heresy the main element is clearly the fully responsible resistance (*pertinacia*), the formal conscious error freely chosen. Later the accent shifts more onto the element of the objective ground for certainty in the idea of faith, whereas the nature of heresy is determined essentially by the purely logical situation of an objective contrariety to a truth of faith (material error), and therefore independent of the subjective state of mind and any historical, factual consideration.

---

[1] A. Lang, "Der Bedeutungswandel der Begriffe 'fides' und 'haeresis' und die dogmatische Wertung der Konzilsentscheidungen von Vienne und Trient," in *Münchener theologische Zeitschrift* 4 (Munich, 1953), p. 134.

Thus it is not surprising that even at the Council of Trent the ideas of "*fides*," "*haeresis*," and "dogma" are still indeterminate in meaning. "Dogma" is primarily a fixed rule, a certain truth or an established fact, and it is even used for the traditions of the Church and for Church disciplines. Their "certainty" resides primarily in the fact that they do not tempt one to anything which is against faith and morality. Thus "dogma" is determined essentially by the reliability of a fixed consciousness of belief. For example, a canon was called a "*dogma fidei*" even if the material of the canon did not belong to the "*depositum fidei*" in our sense, or at least was not regarded as belonging to the deposit of faith. Even if the decisions were based as well on the insight of the general infallibility of the whole Church, that still does not mean that a revealed truth was being directly proclaimed. "The chief characteristic of a '*dogma fidei*' or a canon with an anathema at Trent was precisely the universality with which a truth of the Church was stated."[2]

It is to be noted that when theology first started to reflect on the nature of dogma, faith, and infallibility, these ideas were used far more freely and more generally than they are now. Accordingly, these key words were also far more flexible, so that they became involved concretely in the particular situation of ecclesiastical and dogmatic history and were qualified by it. At Trent, dogma was the equivalent of "*pertinere ad fidem*," and that meant in those days "*esse contra positiones Lutheranorum*."[3] More exact references and the consequences for dogmatic theology which follow from these facts can easily be found elsewhere.

[2] P. Fransen, Schol 27 (1952), p. 556.
[3] Thus Fransen, *Ephemerides Theologicae Lovanienses* 29 (Bruges, 1953), p. 661, note 7.

31

2. MODERN INTELLECTUAL HISTORY
AND THE FATE OF THE CATHOLIC IDEA OF DOGMA

The shift of accent and the change of perspective in the use of the concepts *"fides,"* "dogma," and so forth became inevitable with the challenge of the Reformation. At first, the reformers did not deny that one can arrive at binding pronouncements within the Church and that the truth of the Bible can be arrived at only by a painful struggle with errors and confusions. However much Luther appealed *directly* to Scripture in his important theological breakthroughs (see, for example, the doctrine of justification), he still accepted the Trinitarian and Christological dogma of the old Church as binding.

Yet at the heart of Reformation thought another attitude towards Scripture was growing. According to this view, Scripture is not merely the source and the norm of all Christian discourse, doctrine, and preaching, but it is also the ultimate authority that can be appealed to. Hence all dogmatic statements are, for Protestant theology, binding only at one remove, that is, after it has been shown whether and to what degree dogmas open the way to the immediate teaching of Scripture. It is assumed that Scripture is so clear as to be its own interpretation. "Orthodoxy" takes Scripture as the basis of its dogmatics, for according to the old Protestant doctrine of verbal inspiration it is directly and exclusively identical with the word of God. Since early Protestant orthodoxy—at least in the opinion of a majority of Protestant theologians today—did not preserve the principle of Luther's demolition of the basic "metaphysical" structure of dogma and so itself proceeded "dogmatically" as a kind of Protestant scholasticism, it had to be broken down in the course of the further development of early Protestant theology.

We could also point to numerous other elements in the history of the Church, and many intellectual developments from the fourteenth to nineteenth centuries, in order to demonstrate why the *Catholic* idea of dogma itself underwent a change of meaning even though at the same time it was influenced by an extreme resistance to this break-up and by an attempt to establish more clearly the validity and unique structure of dogma. This change in meaning was possible because of a change in perspective, for the early and especially the medieval Church lived *in the middle* of tradition. Its consciousness, perhaps not explicitly developed but nonetheless effective, of its close relation to the fathers of faith scarcely ever required that the question of tradition be raised. Admittedly, this is a rather simplified view: the *filioque* controversy and, for example, the modes of interpreting *"auctoritates"* in St. Thomas could be used to prove the opposite. Yet it is valid to say of this whole epoch of the Church's history that fundamentally it lived in an almost automatic harmonious relationship with tradition. Basically, the goals were the same as those of the Fathers.

It is against this background that we must see almost everything that was said above about the idea of "dogma," viz. in St. Thomas. The unspecific and not yet fixed usage of the word "dogma" and its equivalents is only the expression of this situation. That had to change the moment that this belief was attacked at the root, in its hidden certainty, reliability, and automatic force, when the new and dangerous heresies emerged at the beginning of the thirteenth century—the new positions of nominalism and, above all, the Reformation and its precursors. Faith must first make sure of itself if it desires

33

to affirm itself as self-sufficient. Thus the question is raised of the objective limitations of *fides divina*, of the theological degree of certainty of the *indirecte credenda*, of the meaning of theological conclusions, and so forth. But that is, in a sense, only the first and more internally theological and technical side of this debate with the new understanding of faith. The Reformation and the modern intellectual movements which, rightly or wrongly, regard themselves as following from it, compel Catholic theology explicitly to raise the question of the nature of the teaching office within the community of faith, or of the value of the concept of conceptual statements contained in dogmatic formulations, and so forth.

It would be an enormous undertaking to pursue the course of modern Catholic theology against this background, though as a result we might be able to see the historical justification and necessity of many aspects of late scholasticism and the "theology of the schools" which have become strange and unintelligible to us.

It was not until the eighteenth century, after a theology of the teaching office had been developed in the sixteenth century, that a fixed use of the word "dogma" emerged. Dating from the end of the seventeenth century, the Jansenists, Gallicans, Regalists, Febronianists, and rationalists sought to reduce the power of conciliar decisions and of papal infallibility, and to regard these primarily as purely disciplinary in intention. All of this also added to the need to clarify the meaning of the word "dogma"—a clarification which, when it came, was perhaps inevitably completely one-sided. It is not at all easy to trace the actual path towards this clarification, and here we will present this conceptual advance only in its final official form, namely, in the concept of dogma defined by Vatican I.

34

3. THE CONCEPT OF DOGMA OF VATICAN I

At the First Council of the Vatican the Church repeated what had already been said by Vincent of Lérin: that revelation is not the product of the mind of man, but is a treasure entrusted by the Lord to his bride, that she may preserve it faithfully and explain it infallibly. But whereas Vincent understood dogmas as the doctrines of faith entrusted to the Church (*depositum divinum*), Vatican I distinguished more clearly between "*depositum*" and "*dogma.*" "The *depositum* is the epitomy of the revelation entrusted to the Church, whereas dogmas are the authentic and authoritative infallible proclamation of the word of God by the Church or the determination of the meaning of a particular revealed truth, *sollemni iudicio*" (J. R. Geiselmann).

This is the change in meaning, and it is made clear by the circumstances of intellectual history and the corresponding measures taken by the Church. A clearer differentiation between *depositum* and *dogma* was necessary simply because the statements of Scripture, of the traditional symbols, and of the doctrine imparted therein, were no longer sufficient for theological and ecclesiastical discussion and debate. That is seen very clearly already in the medieval version of the idea of the "*articulus fidei*," which, especially since Lateran IV, was not too closely tied to the individual statements of the symbol, but for a time even included "*transubstantio*" among the articles, thus ensuring for this doctrine the greatest possible validity.

The history of the above word shows already that the Catholic doctrine of faith must not be slavishly attached to the pure *word* "dogma," nor does it need to be. Of course, it will not simply dismiss an idea which has so grown into its

historical religious consciousness. Even if most doctrinal textbooks give a one-sided presentation of the idea of dogma, that
still does not mean that the essential thing is the authoritative
statement of the Church's teaching office. Gerhard Ebeling's
remark that the word "dogma" is "perfectly appropriate" [4] as a
description of the Catholic mind may well, as is clear from the
preceding, be two-edged. The "establishment of supreme suitability as a technical term of fixed Church doctrine in the
Catholic mind" is possible only on the condition that the actually decisive and constitutive element in dogma is its authoritative nature, that is, the authoritative *"proponere"* of the
"credenda tamquam divinitus revelata," irrespective of many
other elements which are no less constitutive.

Moreover, there are two separate and only juxtaposed kinds
of authority posited: the authority of the word of God, and
the authority of the teaching office which supports and veri-
fies this authority. Only a fuller and more profound treatment
of the *actual* Catholic ideas of dogma, teaching office, authority, and so on, could provide a convincing answer to Ebeling's
objections. Thus, for example, in the use of "infallibility" not
only must the juridical aspect be seen, but also the charismatic
basis, the inner connection of this infallibility with the
Church's life of faith, the infallibility of the total Church and
of the total episcopate *in credendo,* and so forth. Yet even our
historical observations concerning the meaning of dogma
showed that earlier epochs of dogmatic theology by no means
thought in the one-sided categories which Ebeling depicts
them as being. But it would be a misunderstanding to regard
the *necessary* decisions of Vatican I as merely a *logical narrow-
ing* of meaning.

The word of God is divine, absolute, inexhaustible; but

---

[4] See G. Ebeling, *Wort Gottes und Tradition* (Göttingen, 1964).

dogma in this new sense is a human and finite statement by the Church concerning the *depositum fidei*. This statement is certainly infallible, authoritative, and authentic, especially when it is pronounced by the *magisterium extraordinarium* in a *sollemne iudicium* (in the form of a proclamation by a general council or by a doctrinal decision of the pope). In this case, one speaks of a "definition."

A "definition" is a solemn doctrinal pronouncement by which it is authentically, definitively, and infallibly established that a truth is revealed by God and, as such, must be accepted in divine and Catholic faith. Such a definition is made when the Church's teaching office demands, with the whole weight of its authority, a total and irrevocable acceptance of a truth which it teaches.[5] In this case, the intention of a "definition" can be accepted even if the word *"definire"* is not used. Vice versa, the use of the word *"definire"*[6] is not, by itself, a clear sign of a definition. The term *"definire"* is itself neither unambiguous nor formally necessary in decisions which have the character of a "definition."

In the strict sense, therefore, dogma implies the final decision through a solemn "definition" which has at the same time the quality of a canonical ruling of the Church. Its denial is regarded by the Church as "heresy" and is anathematized.[7] In general, the idea of dogma is seen too much in terms of the so-called extraordinary teaching office, as it is exercised by the general councils and in the *ex cathedra* papal decision. But the ordinary general teaching office of the Church (*"magisterium totius Ecclesiae per orbem dispersae"*) also proclaims a "dogma," if something of *fides divina et catholica* is taught in

[5] See Denzinger 3074; CIC 1223, §3.
[6] See Denzinger 1000, 1300, 691, and so forth. See also what Gasser said at Vatican I about the concept of *"definire"*: Mansi 52, 1316.
[7] *CIC* 1325, §2; 2314, §1.

the unanimous confession of faith of the Church as revealed by God, which demands the absolute assent of faith.[8]

Thus the two essential elements in the idea of dogma, as we have seen, are: first, the express and definitive declaration by the Church that a certain statement is a revealed truth—this declaration does not necessarily require an explicit "definition"; and second, the inter-relatedness of this expressed truth to the divine, official, and public Christian revelation (see by way of contrast, for example, so-called private revelation), and thus the fact that it is contained in the word of God as it comes to us in Scripture and/or tradition. The nature of dogma is clearly stated in the declaration by Vatican I concerning the object of *fides divina et catholica:* "Moreover, by divine and Catholic faith are to be believed all those things which are contained in the written or handed-on word of God and which are also put forth by the Church, whether by her solemn declaration or by her ordinary and universal teaching authority, to be believed as divinely revealed." [9] This is the

---

[8] J. S. Drey distinguishes here between a *"Dogma tacitum"* (the Church's unanimous declaration of faith) and a *"dogma declaratum"* (the solemn decisions by the Church). One might also call the dogmas of the extraordinary teaching office "formal" dogmas, in contrast to "material" dogmas. The form of the statement about material dogmas is still relatively free and open, if only the actual contents are correctly reproduced. It is still theologically an open question how precisely one can distinguish between the dogma proclaimed by the regular teaching office and other doctrine which is not presented, or not yet presented, expressly as having been revealed by God. It is to be noted here what *CIC* 1323, §3 maintains: *"Declarata seu definita dogmatice res nulla intelligitur, nisi id manifeste constiterit."* The concrete act of Christian faith naturally can never be limited merely to formal dogmas. These dogmas themselves can be truly personally understood and lived as part of the life of the Church only if they are taken in their inter-relatedness with similar insights, assents, and attitudes. Thus an exact differentiation is not of great significance and perhaps is not even possible (see Denzinger 2880, 2322, 3407 f., 3503, 3884).

[9] Denzinger 3011.

description found today, in more or less extended form, in most Catholic theological and dogmatic textbooks.

This description certainly identifies an important basic feature of dogma. But up till the present day this description has been generally regarded almost exclusively as a "definition." That a statement by the "ordinary and universal teaching authority" is also given the title of "dogma" in this description is something of which most people are hardly aware, and which has been too little worked out conceptually by theologians. Certainly, the defined dogmas have a degree of certainty which is higher and, as it were, *absolutely* fulfilled in their formal aspect—a degree of certainty which then also affects the other aspects of dogma, such as divine origin, truth, the duty of faith, immutability, and so forth. Yet it would be a limitation of meaning if one were to regard this formal element alone as the full nature of dogma. The Church has not described exhaustively all the constitutive factors of dogma in the above-quoted statement from Vatican I, and so has not, in the philosophical sense, defined this idea. The dogmatic decisions of the ordinary magisterium have generally, in any case, the somewhat juridical aspect ("dogma" in the Greek sense) of an obligatory belief in contrast to an existing error, that is, they are generally cast in a polemical form.[10] Precisely because of this limitation these defined truths must be brought back into the totality of faith, they must be related to that center of the Christian mystery which the Church proclaims and which "dogma" in the strict sense also serves. It is precisely here that we must not underestimate the infallibility even of the ordinary magisterium in the kerygma, in the liturgy, and in the other testimonies of the living tradition. What we call "dogma"—almost exclusively with our eye

[10] Thus Franzelin at Vatican I. See Mansi 50, 339 B.

39

on defined decisions—remains, without this connection with the whole, in danger of appearing only as a rigid and merely authoritative framework of formulas. This impression is heightened by the superficial use of naked quotations from Denzinger (however valuable such a compilation is in itself), while disregarding the concrete historical context, the intellectual and spiritual context, and the particular "ethos" in which such decisions are embedded. One often obtains a far more complex and lively picture of a "dogma" if one goes back to its actual sources in all their breadth.

It was necessary to make this point in order to demonstrate the limitations that emerge in an historical account of the development in meaning of the word "dogma." Let us remember St. Thomas's definition of it, and his emphasis on the factual instruction in the otherwise unknown truth and reality of God, the call to the obedience of faith which operates in the divine self-revelation, the perspective of the life-giving religious force of dogma, which ultimately has its measure and draws its necessity from hope in eternal life, and so forth. These elements of dogma are not always in evidence in both official and unofficial use of the word, which are too concerned with the purely formal and authoritative aspect. Hence "dogmas" have tended to be regarded largely only from their character as "propositions." This view is clearly taken for granted by Kant when he calls faith the "acceptance of propositions." In order to do away with these narrow interpretations we should have to elaborate a whole philosophy of the proposition and its qualified applicability to a "dogmatic proposition; but for the present, St. Thomas and the tradition he brought to an end may suffice: *"Actus credentis non terminatur ad enuntiabile, sed ad rem."* [11] The act of faith has as its goal and end, not a

---

[11] *Questiones Disputatae*, q. 14, a. 8 ad 5. See also *Summa Theologiae* I, q. 14, a. 14c; II-II, q. 1, a. 2 ad 2.

formula, but the object that the formula is concerned with. A large part of the customary objections to "dogma" were possible only because the defenders of "dogmas" did not enunciate the full and more complex structure of a dogmatic statement.

The more explicit distinction between *depositum fidei* and dogma, which was also implicit in the official text of the Vatican Council, created certain difficulties: it is just because dogmas are human statements about the word of God that their character and inner tension become more apparent. If dogmas, as human insights, also possess "intellectual" character, they still cannot be totally and evidently known, because in their contents they refer to something which is of an origin that is historical and, above all, supernatural and mysterious.

4. THE ORIGIN AND SIGNIFICANCE OF THE CONCEPT OF DOGMA IN MODERNISM

This basic feature can easily lead one to suppose that dogmas are only "negative" delimitations, that is, that they state only what something is not, without seeking, or being able, to make a positive assertion. Such an interpretation would be based on the analogous structure of dogmatic knowledge and especially on the dimensions of *theologia negativa*. These provide at least *one* preliminary condition for seeing dogmas as "symbols," as is expressed above all in modernism.

However, it is extremely difficult to understand what the actual basic aims of modernism was. It is a confusing mixture of post-Kantian philosophy, of a problematic concept of the symbol (Schleiermacher and Spencer), of anti-intellectual pragmatism, and of the fundamental axioms, by no means self-evident, of modern nineteenth-century historical criticism. All of this, together with quite different elements from various areas of (Church) history, make the history and nature of what is designated by the blanket term "modernism" extremely difficult to grasp. Important observations rub shoulders with extravagant and over-simplified pronouncements, and much of modernist thought has the appearance of remarks made *en passant* rather than of thought-out propositions.

The teaching office of the Church compiled a "system" of modernism which it presented in the decisions of the decree "Lamentabili" of 1907, and the immediately following encyclical *Pascendi dominici gregis* of Pius X, which was directed against agnosticism and immanentism.[12] Although not all of the theses which the decree presents as modernistic can be found in unambiguous form in the writings of individual representatives of the movement, still, at the level of systematic theological reflexion, it points out a number of errors which served, at least potentially, as a basis for the general movement of reform. At the same time, however, it must be noted that many of the problems which modernism raised (the relation between the supernatural character of dogma and its historical manifestation, between dogma which is valid by virtue of the authority of the Church and critical historical exegesis, the place of tradition, and so forth) still have not been solved in a way which can stand up to the questions and challenges of the modern mind. The lack of good monographs on modernism compels us to attempt a brief outline which touches on the concept of dogma held by Loisy.[13]

Modernism directed its first attack against the statement by

[12] See Denzinger 3101-3466; 3475-3500.
[13] See also E. Poulat, *Histoire, dogme et critique dans la crise moderniste*, I (Tournai, 1962); R. Scherer, "Modernismus," in *Lexikon für Theologie und Kirche*, VII (1962), pp. 513-516; R. Aubert, "Modernismus," in *Staatslexikon 6*, III (Freiburg, 1960), pp. 794-801.

Harnack and Sabatier that the dogmatic authority of the Church had been demolished theologically by Luther, scientifically by Galileo, and finally in general by the "historical method." For example, Loisy strongly opposed the view that dogma is merely a petrified formula which, as a complete and absolutely perfect expression of supernatural reality, leads a heavenly existence that is quite independent of all human thinking. Fidelity to tradition does not consist in a static adherence to what has been handed down; the preservation of the faith is not the same thing as the domination of mere formulas. Dogma and revelation are profoundly marked by the duality between transcendent truth and doctrines which emerge concretely in history. The unsurpassable transcendence of this truth produces inevitably a certain degree of relativity in human knowledge; the fact of the development of doctrine within a religious community is the cause of the relativity of the truth that is expressed imperfectly in human words.

This "historical relativity" shows the incessant endeavor of the believing mind to grasp these ideas of supernatural reality which cannot but be inadequately understood by our human intelligence—and to adapt itself to the ever-changing situation of human thinking. The divine itself remains unapproachable and indefinable; dogma itself is only the symbol of reality. The *truth* of a dogma is divine and unchangeable in origin and substance; but we have only the *image* of this truth in our minds. Thus dogma does not have for us an "objective content." Dogma exists only as a function: it must preserve harmony between religious faith and scientific development. The living faith itself demands this constant striving to understand, which is the achievement of individual men and of a collective within a tradition, the continuity of which is guaranteed by the religious community itself. In this sense, the infallibility of

43

the Church, as the concrete sociological form of this religious community, is absolutely necessary, for it is the only thing that makes possible the synthesis of the two facts, so often apparently in contradiction, of an absolute religious faith on the one hand and the inevitable relativity of its symbols on the other. This agreement cannot be guaranteed by the decrees of an authority, but through the good will and the preparedness of precisely those men who are concerned with knowledge and who together reveal a general situation of the Catholic mind, which may be described as the attitude of the Church towards knowledge.

The genesis of dogma begins from a supernatural intuition and a religious experience which can never be expressed in a way that is sufficient for all times. This religious experience is the only way to the content of faith itself. The development of the dogmatic statement begins when this experience is received in faith. If faith is the awareness of God at work in the human consciousness, this consciousness leads to the growth of dogma on the pattern of a purely natural process, whereby, as becomes necessary, agreement with the scientific knowledge of a particular time is sought by means of a more explanatory interpretation, or dogmatic formulas and articles of faith are used in an endeavor to present faith in the major positions of its development. Hence dogma itself is variable; it does not follow the law of a truth which is crystallized in dead formulas, but the movement of the manifold life of history, ever impelled anew by the "religious sense" and "need," always acquired afresh by man according to the constantly changing positions of his intellectual life. Loisy observed such great variations between the original contents of the Gospel and the later formulations of Catholic dogma that he regarded this development largely as a "surrogate." The original meaning of Scripture is arrived at by a "criticism" of its documents. The other "interpretations which have evolved" within the historical life of the Church are different from it.[14]

The Church saw in such views, which were the product of many different influences, a danger to the true idea of revelation, of the unchangeability and supernatural character of faith and dogma. In fact, the equipment of these theologians for entering upon a debate with the modern mind was inadequate in the choice of the appropriate intellectual tools and conceptual categories, and perhaps also in the requisite familiarity with the *real* and basic indispensable statements of a rich Catholic tradition that is not always fully intelligible. This fact is also reflected possibly in the at times almost naïve assurance with which their views on the meaning of Catholic dogma are formulated, which does not suggest much awareness of the tremendous difficulties of such an undertaking. Nevertheless, "modernism" may justly claim to have pointed to the pressing need for this debate, and the actual decision taken in the modernist crisis was, despite the necessity for an official reaction by the Church, a tragedy of the first order within it. Considering that, despite these authoritative measures, the Church's doctrinal office held that there were still grounds for further warnings in the encyclical *Humani generis* of Pius XII, we find in the theology of this period a notable caution in the face of these questions and a somewhat sterile reserve in the face of

[14] An article by Eduard Le Roy, "What is Dogma?" in the periodical *La Quinzaine* (1905), presented basically the same point of view. The idea of dogma must be freed from an old-fashioned intellectualism which can only harm the Church. Dogma has primarily only a negative meaning. "God is a person" means only that one cannot say that God is not a person. In the positive field, however, the essence of dogma lies in the area if action. It means less an intellectual illumination of the mind than a guide to the proper religious attitudes and to Christian action, so that ultimately the purely pragmatic viewpoint sets the ethical and practical elements in revelation above its conceptual and intellectual importance.

the work still to be done. Perhaps one may say that the theology of recent years appears to be facing these problems with more courage.

B. The Kinds of Dogma

We must still say something about the different types of dogma, inasmuch as the differences are not covered in an account of theological epistemology and theological qualifications. Dogmas can be divided according to various criteria. In the preceding we have distinguished—as does the Church—between formal and (merely) material dogmas, or, as J. S. Drey calls them, "*dogma declaratum*" and "*dogma tacitum*." In terms of content and range, we may distinguish between general and fundamental truths of Christian faith (articles of faith, fundamental articles, *regula fidei*) and special dogmas. Although the equal value of all dogmas, from a formal point of view, must be emphasized against so-called fundamentalism, simply because they have been guaranteed by God and finally pronounced by the Church, the above distinction is meaningful in that dogmas possess a significance for salvation which varies according to the divine truth expressed by them. This is seen in canon law from the fact that not every heretical denial of a dogma is branded by the whole of Christendom as "apostasy." Moreover, there is a further distinction in terms of content that can be made among the fundamental dogmas: those dogmas that are necessary for salvation and those that are not, which is to be decided according to whether they must expressly be believed (*in necessitas medii—necessitas praecepti*) in order to lead to salvation, or whether a so-called "*fides implicita*" is sufficient.

Further distinctions can be made according to their relation to reason. Pure dogmas are those which can be known *only* through revelation, that is, which are "mysteries" in the narrowest sense; mixed dogmas are those whose contents can also be known, in varying degrees, by natural reason. If we may say that pure truths of reason which are self-authenticating may still be *believed* by the same person, then the so-called mixed dogmas are also different from the rational truth which has the "same" content. As dogmas they are grasped out of the totality of revelation and of belief in salvation and are understood in faith. They offer their truth within the framework of supernatural mysteries (the full meaning of this framework would have to be further gone into), they stand in unique relationships with pure dogmas, and so forth. We should have also to inquire how far and, above all, in what sense it could be said that there is here still a material "sameness." Such dogmas cannot be denied in their necessity, however much one may inwardly resist having to include truths of reason within the immediate area of "dogma." Such dogmas are, in fact, an indication that the revelation of God really *meets* man, that is, really is adjusted to the circumstances of man's existence. This also implies that "dogma" is not merely an abstract "truth" which is fixed in itself through theological reflexion as a certainty of faith, but that true dogma translates itself automatically into the wide area of the life of faith. The statements of faith are—against all fideist, supernaturalist, and pietist tendencies—not statements which are relative to some special and limited area of man's life, and achieve their effect only there; but they are, as statements of *faith,* aimed at the *total* reality of human life.

The question whether "dogma" and "defined" statements are identical or not, whether apart from dogma there can be other truths guaranteed and defined with absolute authority by the Church, and what kind of truths these would be (so-

47

called "dogmatic facts," mere "faith of the Church") will be treated elsewhere.

This lengthy account of the history of the word "dogma" was necessary in order to avoid over-simplifications and to demonstrate the fundamental openness of these central ideas. We must now proceed to discuss briefly the objective necessity of the idea of "dogma," especially insofar as "dogma" is related to "kerygma."

III. FROM KERYGMA TO DOGMA

A. The Objective Necessity of the Transition from Kerygma to Dogma

The question of the scriptural basis for the idea of dogma can be answered in many ways. However, we must avoid arguing on the basis only of a few texts in order to provide a subsequent justification for the development of specific theological statements in the history of dogma and the Church. It is not enough, for example, to quote the words "He who hears you hears me" in order to prove on the basis of such scriptural passages the need for the obedience of faith in relation to specifically dogmatic pronouncements.

1. THE TENSION BETWEEN BIBLICAL AND DOGMATIC THEOLOGY

Arguments such as these primarily fail to take account of the objective and historical tension between the kerygmatic, linguistic, and conceptual forms of Scripture and the mode of dogmatic and speculative statements which are partially cast in a particular ontological language. What is today gathered together in the formal idea of "biblical theology" originated historically in an open or latent opposition to anything like "dogmatics." From its beginning biblical theology has had the tendency to move away from interposing speculation and to

49

return to the purer sources of unadulterated theological knowledge. If this move away from dogmatism was strongly influenced by the Reformation, the history of modern Protestantism shows at the same time that the slogans "biblical theology" or "kerygma" contributed to the dethroning of dogmatic thinking. The now popular contrast between the original purity of the Gospel and the secondary ontological language of dogmatic theology which grew up on Hellenistic soil can no longer be presented today in the violently antithetical manner of M. Werner, Harnack and his school, and others. The unquestionable difference between the two, however, in view of the various misuses of dogmatic ways of thinking, presents a task to be performed, a task which any treatment of an objectively argued transition from kerygma to dogma cannot ignore.

2. THE INNER CONNECTION BETWEEN KERYGMA AND DOGMA IN SCRIPTURE

We may approach the subject of the inner connection between kerygma and dogma as witnessed in Scripture itself by pointing out the presence of already fixed confessions of faith in the New Testament itself (see, for example, 1 Corinthians 15, 3-5; Romans 1, 3 f.; 1 Thessalonians 1, 9-10, and so forth), which are themselves of different types, having either a solemn, liturgical, and hymnic character of a more prosaic, catechetical, doctrinal flavor (see "acclamation" and "confession" in Philippians 2, 5-11). If one also sees in these confessional traditions not merely "kerygmatic summaries" or "dry schemata" which are at best only starting points for explicit theological discourse, and thus are only basic pieces of a catechetical and parenetical tradition to which one accords only a practical value, on closer examination a one-sided appeal to these confessional formulas is not without its problems. In fact, they are by no means homogeneous in their theological concepts; they do not even present the same material statements in the framework of the same theological perspective, and betray their descent from very diverse local tradition and *Sitz im Leben*.

The importance of these traditions of confessional statements for dogmatic theology must rather be sought in the fact that the early Christian theological thought which they contain is based on common credal formulas which at the time of the pre-literary composition of the gospels were coordinating points for this creation of the "Gospel" and both consciously and unconsciously influenced and marked the kerygma (see, for example, the function of 1 Corinthians 15, 3 ff. for Paul). We shall have to return later to this significance of the credal tradition.

"Tradition" altogether was equally important in the formation of the gospels, without its having to possess already the binding character of credal formulas. Its importance is seen most clearly, in varying degrees, in the synoptists, but modern scholarship has shown also that in Paul and John the material from tradition plays a very important role.

Another way of understanding dogmatic thought, in the wider sense, within the New Testament is seen in the interpretation of the Old Testament by the original community. This interpretation of "Scripture" begins with an event of New Testament revelation history and the credal utterances which belong to it. It is the Christ event which gives the Old Testament its true and profound significance. We are unable here to go into the hermeneutic conditions of such an interpretation, the proper understanding of the "proof from Scripture" used in the New Testament, and the different meaning of the word "scripture" in the Old and New Testaments, but the main thing is the sheer fact of the possibility of this interpretation which undoubtedly contains "dogmatic" traces.

A striking example of the dogmatic interpretation of Scripture within the New Testament itself is also the fact that certain statements of Jesus (see, for example, the prophecies of suffering, the sayings referring to the Son of man, and so forth) are interpreted in the light of the faith in the Messiah which came after the Resurrection. The proclamation of Jesus and Christ in the gospels (especially in the fourth gospel), which is determined by the post-Easter situation, has, in fact, been interpreted in a very different sense as a "dogmatic veneer," but it is agreed today in "critical" circles of exegesis that critical historical research is not sufficient to illuminate the "historical" Jesus—who would, after all, have unique claims to validity, and yet by being narrowed down in this way would have been reduced to a pallid figure. Thus Ernst Käsemann, for example, maintains in his somewhat exaggerated polemic against Jeremias that the latter also melted off the dogmatic varnish from the original picture with the fire of an importunate scholarship "in order to prove ultimately how impregnable to fire it was."[1] The radical nature of this and also of opposite endeavors shows only too clearly that this sort of "dogmatic" vestigia cannot be removed from the New Testament without making the picture of Jesus Christ completely colorless and insignificant in every way.

It is not our purpose here to draw positive conclusions from these various facts for a possible interpretation of the dogmatic element in the New Testament itself (see below), but to show that there are important essential elements in

[1] E. Käsemann, *Exegetische Versuche und Besinnungen*, II (Göttingen, 1964), p. 41.

the New Testament which preclude dismissing as mistaken any statement, however cautious, about dogma being a fact within the New Testament.

On a point of method, one might legitimately ask the question here why this interpretation of the New Testament, emphasizing as it does the dogmatic motifs within it, should still be necessary *today*. The answer would have to be that, in the light of contemporary "faith consciousness" and preaching of the Church, the need for a translation of the Christian message into "modern terms" (which is already shown as necessary by the New Testament itself) shows that by pointing out the dangers of such an undertaking (adapting and falsifying what has been revealed), we might gain the proper criteria for judging such attempts, which can proceed only out of the harmony of contemporary religious consciousness with the faith and doctrine of all ages and all generations of the Church and its experiences in interpreting the "Gospel." The apostolic tradition and the teaching office of the Church are then only elements in the Church's understanding of the original word. This way contains the essential elements which any discussion of the justification of dogmatic work within Catholic theology must presuppose. However, any profounder attempt at justification cannot ignore recent objections which question the very foundation of the dogmatic approach, on the ground that the great variations within the New Testament kerygma do not permit one to see any unity in Scripture (and hence in the Church). Käsemann's words have become famous: "The New Testament canon as such is not the basis of the Church's unity. On the contrary, in the form in which the historian encounters it, it is the basis of the diversity of the Church's denominations." This statement that the unity of the Church simply cannot be proved, and its denial of the right of any one confession to an absolute claim, also destroys the right to make, and even the possibility of making, binding dogmatic decisions. If one does not let oneself be deterred by this sharply one-sided formulation from considering the genuine question which it poses for a Catholic theologian, and if one is prepared to tackle the problems raised by the notion of the variability of the New Testament kerygma, then the idea of the dogmatic and the transition from kerygma to dogma can only emerge more clearly.

3. THE RANGE OF VARIATION IN THE NEW TESTAMENT KERGYMA AND IN EARLY CHRISTIAN "THEOLOGY"

The variability appears already in language when, for example, we find in the New Testament doctrine of salvation a number of ideas which refer to various elements in very different ways: "forgiveness," "healing," "sealing," "justification," "sanctification," "purification," "election," "redemption," "transformation," "rebirth," "conquest," "life," and so forth. There is no one formal or material concept in the New Testament itself that subsumes all these soteriological ideas and motifs. Many different aspects of the nature of the saving act of God towards his people are presented in the New Testament. If one single aspect is made the dominant idea, then the consequences are obvious: over-interpretations, ideas pressed too far, the isolation of themes which are interwoven, dry schemata, and so forth. The range of variation automatically prevents narrowness, blunting, hackneyed and external interpretation, and lack of understanding. But the many different forms of the early Christian kerygma not only have these advantages, but also involve many contradictions and obscurities. Formulations by Paul and by James seem to be in opposition to one another (see, for example, Romans 3, 28 and James 2, 24; also Galatians 7, 12; Romans 7, 12; Matthew 5, 17 f.; Romans 10, 4). The eschatological statements of the synoptics, and of Paul, and John seem at first sight incompatible. We are more familiar with the questions concerning the moment of the parousia, the problem of its early expectation, the statements about the offices of the Church, the fundamental differences in the accounts of the Last Supper. It would be quite easy to extend the list of these objections. The whole problem of so-called "early Catholicism" resides in the extension of this line.

However, it is not our purpose to investigate the reason for these "contradictions." Our question is only: how far can such a variety of forms in the early Christian kerygma be the norm of the Church? W. Marxsen replies that "Whoever is not determined to harmonize the New Testament by force, in reinterpreting what is said to the point at which it no longer means what it says, but is prepared to take what is said as what is meant, must come to the conclusion that the New Testament, the early tradition, is not suitable, on grounds of content, to be a norm for the doctrine of the Church; for only that which is a unified statement in itself can be a norm."[2]

Although the Catholic theologian regards the unity of Scripture and Church to be, in a manner, settled, in that Scripture is the inspired and authentic word of God that has been formulated in the canon of the New Testament, he is still able to acknowledge the limited and fragmentary structure of the actual theology of the New Testament writings. Theological statements are made in the New Testament, different motifs are sounded, and then there is suddenly profound silence once more. It has often been pointed out that there are great differences in the language, form, origin, and basis of the living

[2] *Einheit der Kirche?* (Witten, 1964), p. 15.

life of the New Testament community. Modern scholarship, concerned as it is with the history of the compilation and tradition of the gospels, has clearly shown the variety of theological backgrounds and points of view which determined the selection, elaboration, and arrangement of the traditional material. The theology of the different epochs of salvation history in Luke and the theology of the epiphany in Mark are cases in point. But all these particular theologies are ultimately only fragments of one "theology," which reveals with full clarity the limited historical character of these "occasional writings." An idea is rarely pursued into all its concrete ramifications; inner relationships are not always clear; and in particular, these fragments, so often diverse in content and form, also differ markedly in the degree and depth of their theological thought. "The idea of one biblical theology which grows out of a single root and maintains itself in an unbroken continuity is a wishful dream and a phantom."[3] Whoever does not care to subscribe wholly to this uncompromising view must still admit that, for example, Jewish-Christian and Hellenistic theology are quite different. The only question is whether one may start according to Käsemann from the idea—and the demand which it implies—of an easily accessible, obvious, and unified theology behind, or even present within, the New Testament. But that means that the fact of such a pluralist and fragmentary theology is not particularly important because this fact immediately requires interpretation or already brings its own interpretation with it. The mere fact, looked at by itself, can certainly be understood in various ways.

The hidden problems underlying this situation involve a most comprehensive basic principle of revelation: the difference between "Scripture" and "Gospel," in the sense that

[3] Käsemann, *op cit.*, p. 27.

Scripture cannot be automatically equated, without further differentiation, with revelation. The pluralism and the variety of the early Christian kerygma show that the inner wealth of revelation operates against arbitrary speculation or dogmatic fixing. The sum of individual passages of Scripture and of individual testimonies is not "the Gospel." The historical nature of revelation is manifested precisely in this ineluctable difference between "Scripture" and "Gospel." Even if this tension brings out other elements when one is attempting to justify dogma by means of the New Testament, it now clearly imposes caution on the search and will prevent one's being able to take the New Testament simply as the first Christian dogmatics. Scripture cannot be merely the jumping-off point for theological work, providing at best only the "material." The important question is how to determine what the "Gospel behind the gospels" really says. Do not the many variations reflect *one* thing only—but how can we approach this "thing"?

Before we try to answer this question, however, we must enquire how far we are in fact acquainted with the actual differences in early Christianity and its theology. We know so little in this field, and the hypotheses that have been made are inevitably so vague and uncertain (see, for example, Lohmeyer's distinction between a Jerusalem tradition and a tradition based in Galilee; the demand for a specifically Judaistic-Hellenistic Christianity which would overcome the narrowness of the rigid system of the original Palestine community versus Hellenistic Christianity; the different descriptions, both in time and place, of the Jewish Christian—right down to the Ebionites), that there are at any rate no compelling conclusions which may be drawn from them, as though early Christianity had been a collection of diverse "denominations." In such depictions, modern interpretative models are often used anachronistically, which serves only to obscure the relative strangeness of this period. It is equally not permissible to seek the unity of Scripture that one desires only in fixed formulations, or in statements of any kind. The criteria which are needed to ensure, for example, "total harmony" between all statements would themselves need some measure according to which such a test could be carried out.

4. THE PROBLEM OF THE THEOLOGICAL UNITY OF SCRIPTURE

The ways pursued in order to find some kind of measure for the unity of Scripture may be described briefly as attempts to overcome the dissatisfaction with the New Testament canon as it stands by interpreting it according to a particular objective canon or setting up another formal principle of unity. Statements by Luther may be quoted to justify the introduction of such an objective canon: "*Scripturea est non contra, sed pro Christo intelligenda, ideo vel ad eum referenda, vel pro vera scriptura non habenda.*"[4] "*Si adversarii scripturam urserint contra Christum, urgemus Christum contra scripturam.*"[5] "*Si utrum sit amittendum, Christus vel lex, lex est amittenda, non Christus.*"[6] This extraordinarily important approach to the interpretation of Scripture was not, in the opinion of modern Protestant theology, worked out by Luther in all its far-reaching consequences. It is only *now* that the task emerges of straightfoward critical work on the text, in which, for E. Käsemann, for example, justification by faith alone is the theological yardstick. "We must be prepared to let the individual scriptural text say what it says, only we

---

[4] *Werke. Kritische Gesamtausgabe* (Weimar edition), 39 f.; 47, 3f.
[5] *Ibid.*, 39, 1; 47, 19f.
[6] *Ibid.*, 39, 1; 47, 23f.

must not then say that it is automatically the word of God! For the word of God is that alone which declares and communicates the will of God apparent in the crucified Christ."[7] In contrast to this critical selective principle the Catholic attitude to the canon and tradition is described as "legally egalitarian."[8] Only one might ask how the "matter" which is the concern of Scripture in fact becomes evident. In order to escape the hermeneutic assistance of tradition, G. Ebeling interprets the "*sola Scriptura*" of the Reformation as meaning that the implicit "committal to the clarity of Scripture does not involve the clarity of every single text and therefore not the lack of contradiction within the literal statements, but the clarity of what the Gospel scripture is about."[9] This only puts off the problem, for the "clarity of what the Scripture is about" is—apart from its being conveyed in language—no more self-evident than the clarity of the text. The recent history of Protestant theology (including the debate concerning demythologization and the turn to fundamental hermeneutics) shows precisely that the "argument" concerning this "matter" of Scripture by no means produces that clarity and in fact must even be reproached for abandoning essential elements and aspects of this "matter" of Scripture, reducing it to overformal categories.

Ebeling is certainly right when he maintains, against Käsemann, that to speak of "contradictions" in the canon is somewhat hasty,[10] that the observation of correct details and the emphasis on the manifold nature of the early Christian kerygma should not lead one to generalize about it, and so forth. Even

[7] Ebeling, *Das Wesen des christlichen Glaubens* (Tübingen³, 1963), p. 45; ET *The Nature of Faith* (Philadelphia, 1962).
[8] Ebeling, *Wort Gottes und Tradition,* pp. 151f.
[9] *Ibid.,* p. 152.
[10] See *ibid.,* pp. 144-154.

more important is his point that the difference between the
various denominations and hence the question of the unity
of Scripture cannot be understood only in terms of the different interpretations of *particular* single texts, but that at the
profoundest level it is primarily fundamental hermeneutic
differences (re language, how truth and reality are understood,
historical allegiances, and so forth) which create the diverg-
ences and which concern basically *all* the texts. The point of
controversy is not the appeal to many texts which differ one
from another (are "contradictory"), but much more signifi-
cantly the diverse interpretations of the *same* texts.

Biblical theology which is aware of its task is already concerned with examining the contents of revelation and even
with expressing them in a special way (see ideas such as
"eschatology," "salvation history," "sacrament"), because it
cannot simply reproduce the words and concerns of Scripture,
keeping to the particular theological language of the individual
writers, but must itself offer an appropriate development of
New Testament theology in its theological intentions: a full
understanding of the inner relationships of the contents of
revelation, inasmuch as they can be understood from the understanding of faith within the New Testament itself. The
problem is that it is an open question whether this kind of
clarification marks the end of the process of interpretation or
whether it has to be continued. A naïve biblical theology, in
the sense of a formal general concept, is unequipped from the
start to be even aware of the problem of thus presenting theological contents as they appear to the religious thinking of the
New Testament.

Other criteria which have been applied in order to find the
actual "center" of Scripture are too limited in their point of
view. If Scripture is regarded as "kerygmatic unity" (see the
theological work of H. Diems), that is, if it is seen as a unified

account of salvation history, then this approach has grave limitations. "Kerygmatic unity" is in opposition to "doctrinal unity," and all the differences can be explained only too easily by the particular kerygmatic situation. But here the situation becomes too readily the criterion of the Gospel itself, whereas at best it is the occasion of the Gospel and gives it its starting point of attack, but does not impart to it its own character to the extent that the Gospel itself disappears behind the changing situations. "Salvation history" itself is an idea which is being overworked. Is it a kind of theology of history or a particular element within Pauline theology? If one sees the "canon within the canon" as an "original kerygma" or a "first testimony,"[11] one lands oneself in endless discussions because, particularly recently, the constructions and attempts and reconstructions of the so-called "original kerygma" have become historically questionable, and because in early times there was probably a relatively large variety of forms (see the discourses of Acts according to the researches of U. Wilckens, E. Haenchen, and others with an exact analysis of 1 Corinthians 15, 3 ff.). The "normative original kerygma" remains problematical, particularly if one looks less at what has actually been said and seeks to discover a preceding system of ideas.

Philology and the history of ideas alone are not enough to solve the basic questions. The mass of the material which has to be worked through becomes ever more unwieldy; even the translation of fundamental scriptural ideas, such as *"dynamis"* as "power," "strength/possibility,"[12] is not without its problems. Exegesis sometimes is forced to give up altogether before the controversial theological questions it raises. Basically, how-

[11] Thus Marxsen, "Kontingenz der Offernbarung oder (und?) Kontingenz des Kanons?", in *NZSTh* 2 (1960), pp. 355ff., esp. p. 363.
[12] See the discussion between Käsemann and Bultmann, *Exegetische Versuche und Besinnungen* II, p. 186, note.

ever, it acknowledges that important differences in hermeneutics create different ways of understanding and that these
are not fully independent and distinguishable from the process
of interpretation itself. Thus, for example, a naïve *"sola Scriptura"* is abandoned.[13] Thus it was that theological elements
were discovered in Paul which had been considered to belong
to the late strata of the New Testament NT canon and generally held to be typically "Catholic."[14] "Modern historical
criticism of Scripture stood for a long time under the shadow
of the view that critico-historical work on Scripture was
dangerous to Catholicism and favorable to Protestantism. But
the exegetical and historical research of the biblical sciences
over recent decades has taken a surprising turn which in many
respects is advantageous to the Catholic view."[15]

The idea of a "factual canon" by which one could measure
the individual statements of different witnesses is problematical
today because this factual center is used critically against
divergent scriptural statements (in contrast to the "rule of
faith" in the older Church and to the *analogia fidei*). The
"spirit of Scripture" itself must be tested. The differentiation
between the spirit and the letter becomes the criterion of the
correct understanding of Scripture. Whenever one imagines
that God has been misused and captured in a statement declared by him, but heard by man, the spirit is brought into
play and a letter posited. Even if the "spirit" is not played off
against the "word," and one is aware that "spirit" also needs
to be interpreted, that the "spirit" is not just the arch-enemy
of all "tradition," the whole unreality of hoping to discover

[13] See Ebeling, *Wort Gottes und Tradition,* p. 149; see also *ibid.,* pp.
91-143.
[14] See *ibid.,* p. 149; see also Käsemann, *Exegetische Versuche und
Besinnungen* II, pp. 239-252 and *passim.*
[15] Ebeling, *Wort Gottes und Tradition,* p. 149.

an actual critical center in Scripture emerges. According to this view, the unity of Scripture is based on a fundamental hermeneutical statement which, it must be maintained, is in harmony with the real spiritual and theological concern of the witnesses (see, for example, the role of Paul and John in Bultmann's demythologization, and belief in justification as the norm of interpretation in Käsemann). Consequently, the unity of Scripture can finally be realized only in the understanding and the spirit of the interpreter and thus it loses its own "objective" unity.

Other attempts to demonstrate unity suffer from the particularity with and in which they are opposed to other guiding ideas and principles of interpretation that could claim at least equally to be an essential element of Scripture. This is then the weakness of the doxological position. The idea of doxology (as represented, for example, by E. Schlink) cannot be the only structural element of the Christian confession of faith. Nor, obviously, can the problem be solved by preferring to the "dogmatic" the modes of statement of the confession of faith (*confessio*), as often happens today in Protestant theology. "It is true that it is part of the nature of the confession of faith that for it to be valid it must be made in full personal responsibility. This means that the appeal to the confession of faith of the Reformation as the authoritative testimony of Church doctrine commits one to independent theological work, both in regard to the testing and the present actualization, and hence concrete identification, of traditional Church doctrine."[16] Because the confession of faith is tied to the specific origin of a Church pronouncement of doctrine ("to the exceptional situation of the making of a decision, in which that is expressed afresh which makes the Church the Church, sep-

[16] *Ibid.*, p. 170.

arating off and making it manifest as the concrete Church community"), it does not go through a process of becoming more fixed and differentiated, like Church doctrine. Ebeling sees in this essential difference between dogma and confession of faith the legitimate reason why, for example, in the history of modern Protestantism there have been no notable, clearly formulated statements of faith or doctrine.[17] Hence this fact is not merely a sign of the weakening and the reduction of Church significance, a phenomenon of decadence. Even if one is unable, and does not desire, to agree with these clearly defined views and the consequences that have been drawn from them, these questions present almost insoluble difficulties. As far as the idea of "dogma" is maintained and functions as an idea of relationship (to the proclamation of the Gospel, to revelation, to the God that reveals himself and commands, and so forth), this harmony appears by no means self-evident or even necessarily possible. "The breakdown of the basic idea in *contemporary theology* comes from the fact that it has become more and more narrowly intellectual and has been regarded no longer as a phenomenon of the Church, but in the main as a theological one, as material for scholarly work. In almost all dogmatic pronouncements the reference to the kerygma conceals uncertainty in the understanding of the idea of dogma."[18]

Thus it is not enough to say that the unity of Scripture is the "concern" of revelation and that this has been laid down in dogma. Even the variations in the original Christian kerygma serve basically only *one* thing. "Not that its terminology, but that what it is about may appear and remain evident, this is the important thing. The range of variation prevents abbrevia-

[17] See *ibid.*, pp. 167f.
[18] G. Gloege, "Dogma," in *Die Religion in Geschichte und Gegenpart*[3] II (Tübingen, 1958), p. 223.

tion, limitation, weakening, and failure to understand. And yet the variations continue to reflect in all their prismatic surfaces *one* thing only, and are used by the apostle only insofar as they are capable of doing this."[19] W. Marxsen also points out that in spite of all the different interpretations, for example the different accounts of the Last Supper, it is still only about *one* thing. What then is critical research after, if it upsets the traditional understanding of this dogmatic object of the New Testament? "What is criticized is the use of the New Testament as a recipe book by means of which one is able directly to solve dogmatic questions. What is criticized is the attempt to understand the New Testament writings as *direct* statements to the present. This is also a criticism of that method of using the Bible according to which every denomination considers that it is able to justify its ideas by appealing to the New Testament. The texts *themselves* are not what it is about, but they are the witness to what it is about and are conditioned by the time and situation in which they originated."[20] If, however, the statement "I believe in Jesus Christ" is quoted as the innermost secret of the Christian confession of faith, no one who lays claim to the title of Christian for himself will deny this statement, but immediately a thousand ways of understanding it will present themselves, together with all the Christological controversies of two millenniums and the great question of *who* this man Jesus was.

The history of the Christian faith bears clear witness to the fact that one has to move beyond the words of the Bible. If the systematic theologian only sticks "historically" to the word of Scripture, then he is depriving the original word of its closeness to the present and of its effectiveness. There is no

[19] Käsemann,, "Erwägungen zum Stichwort 'Versöhnungslethre im Neuen Testament'," in *Zeit und Geschichte* (Tübingen, 1964), p. 58.
[20] Marxsen, *op cit.*, pp. 27-28.

such thing as a direct relationship, without any presuppositions, to Scripture—either within theological study or within the simple life of faith—which is able to ignore the history of the Church's appropriation of the Gospel. Whoever pretends that he has no tradition and insists upon a rigid "*sola Scriptura*" is only the more deeply involved in his own origins, origins which have become completely mysterious to him. That the language of the New Testament does not offer any clear guidance on orthodoxy and heresy and that conscientious historical study has worked out philologically that variety is the peculiar characteristic of the early Christian proclamation of the Gospel is unquestionable. It can even be shown that the Christian kerygma and the first beginnings of theology in Scripture itself do not consist in an uncritical reception of fixed religious contents and statements (whether of Jewish, Hellenistic, Gnostic, or any other origin), but in a new interpretation of traditionally received material by connecting it with the historical revelation in Jesus Christ. The particular linguistic formulation which has been handed down cannot be the measure of correct belief. The very holding on to traditional modes of expression often leads, on the contrary, to heresy (as, for example, monophysitism and monotheletism are, according to the latest researches of J. Lebon and others, "heresy" because they refused to undergo a linguistic and conceptual differentiation at a time when the traditional formulas had in fact become ambiguous). That which later "became" heresy may once have been the form and manifestation of a belief that was right in its time (for example, the so-called subordinationist theology of the history of salvation of the second and third centuries and the significance of Nicaea). The flight into tradition and to a pre-given language of absolute validity offers the possibility of new heresies. The development of the Christological thinking of the early Church is proof of this fact. The situation does not change either when "dogmas" are acknowledged. These also share—perhaps in a much greater degree—in the need to make present and actual the Christian message (and just because of that: "dogma" exists in order to translate it ever anew into the different languages the world speaks at different times). Hence it is not the case that Catholic theology maintains that it is Scripture that is unclear or the contents of Scripture in its linguistic form, but that the clear thing is ambiguously and forever the dogmatic interpretation of Scripture. An interpretation of dogma itself is not possible without referring back to its origin, which is why dogma, with all its moving out into translation and differentiation, returns again to the central thing, withdraws from all its polemical involvements, and gathers itself again towards its center, and finds there the criteria to make its differentiations.

Thus we shall make a final attempt to show that "dogma" is the development of the correctly understood contents of Scripture. Many objections concerning the thesis of an exaggerated range of variation in the early Christian kerygma and a legalist-egalitarian understanding of the canon by the Catholic Church may be countered or else require a special examination of the particular facts. Thus, for example, one could show that Catholic theology can still regard the canon as valid in all its parts without being compelled to see the canonical writings as all alike one after the other, like a compendium without any inner tensions within it. One might point out that the Council of Trent still speaks of different gradations of the biblical books. Moreover, the message of the New Testament must not be narrowed down to one single moment, to the neglect of the historical process (for example, the position of the Epistle of James compared to that of the Pauline epistles).

5. THE FUNDAMENTAL OPENNESS OF SCRIPTURE AS A POSSIBLE REFERENCE TO DOGMA

Summing up, one may describe the situation of the New Testament itself in relation to the question of the unity of Scripture and of the Church in the following words of O. Kuss: "The theological unity of the New Testament is neither a fact nor a problem of the New Testament itself . . . the unity of the New Testament does not impose itself as a self-evident result of theological critico-historical research, but is—at least as far as the mode of knowing it is concerned—a reflection of the unity of the hierarchically structured Church of the second century which—in the course of often difficult struggles which continued sporadically until the fourth century—recognized the individual writings with their various theologies as belonging to Scripture."[21] This unity, which also embraces an ultimate lack of contradiction between the various basic ideas and theological motifs, is—seen theologically—undoubtedly a premise connected with the doctrine of the inspiration and canonicity of Scripture, as is shown elsewhere. We can now demonstrate by exegesis that this unity, however obscure it may seem when set against the whole range of the comprehensive universality of Scripture, is still a real thing. For one thing, we can always see in the individual writings of the New Testament a clear tendency to the unity of the Church. Then we can see in the writings of the New Testament that the possibility and the fact of wrong teaching are clearly taken into account; but that undoubtedly means also that the New Testament itself is on the way to a doctrine. Otherwise it would be incomprehensible how and why early Christianity

[21] *Auslegung und Verkündigung* I (Regensburg, 1963), p. 11, note 5.

bases itself on common credal formulas. Finally, let us refer the reader to the works of H. Schlier who has investigated from another point of view "the unity of the Church according to the New Testament."[22] Taking, then, these facts for granted, we shall endeavor to pursue a few lines which were briefly touched on in the preceding discussion.

The scriptural writings themselves were the occasion of their acceptance by the Church, even if the history of this fact is a very long one and the details are not very clear to us. The increasingly numerous written traditions were sorted out, and in the process "the basic and authoritative tradition of the revealed events was made present to the Church."[23] The decision must be accepted in all its importance. It is also recognized by the majority of Protestant theologians as a permanent rule of the Church's life.

Finally, the insight of modern exegesis that the New Testament offers the testimony of the revelation in Jesus Christ already in terms of religious reflexion suggests that the events of revelation themselves did not find their linguistic and conceptual form in any other way than that "as well as faith they aroused reflexion about faith."[24] There is no such thing as a "word of God" which does not appear already as a word that is heard and even *thought* in faith, so that in this sense "revelation" itself as the living self-revelation of God basically and by its very nature requires the hearing and thinking man as the place where it realizes itself and without which it cannot exist. But that also implies that the New Testament itself contains indications concerning reflexion about faith and for covering the possibility of asking further questions by drawing out the lines of its own perspectives.

[22] *Besinnung auf das Neue Testament* (Freiburg, 1964), pp. 178-192.
[23] *Ibid.*, p. 26; see pp. 25-34.
[24] *Ibid.*, p. 26.

It cannot be objected here that this kind of thinking which goes beyond Scripture is abandoning it. This view would be valid only if the formulations, the sayings (or rather the words) and ideas of Scripture were there for their own sake and not for that of the object to which they are referring. Modern phenomenological and hermeneutic investigation (Husserl, Heidegger, H. Lipps, Gadamer) has shown that the word as such—because it is profoundly unconscious and is not itself an object—carries hidden within itself an inner dimension of multiplicity of meaning and a fundamental openness, which in the frequent incompleteness of our speech betokens a linguistic power which activates a more comprehensive totality of meaning, of relations to questions and answers, a totality which cannot be explicitly stated as a whole by the individual subject in any one moment. If, therefore, every word suggests also what it contains that is unsaid, then it carries a superfluity of meaning which is not actually knowable at every moment, a meaning which is revealed only in a history of hermeneutic experience and emerges more openly in language in the course of the dialogue that is history. But this modern idea is basically an old one. For example, at the beginning of the short essay "De natura verbi intellectus" (probably by St. Thomas and to be found among his works) we read: "*Quod verbum cum re dicta per verbum convenientiam habet maiorem in natura sua quam cum dicente, licet in dicente sit ut in subjecto.*" Now if we understand inspiration correctly, we can say that this property of the human word appears most fully in the "word of God in the human mouth," where to a far higher degree an infinity of meaning to be interpreted is presented in a finite way.

That is why it is not a contradiction if the occasional writings of the New Testament which are addressed to specific people make wider and more comprehensive claims. For example, perhaps we do not know exactly for whom St. John's Gospel was written. The Epistle to the Colossians can, and must, be certainly interchangeable with an epistle to Laodicea. In the pastoral epistles the Pauline gospel appears expressly as a "legacy" which God will preserve to the Last Judgment and which Timothy is to preserve as a "pattern of sound words." In these letters we can also see clearly the basis of the possibility of transcending the original statement without abandoning it and also how this transcendence operates. The word in which the events of revelation are expressed and in which they are preserved in the power of the spirit is, if one may so say, an "original word." It is spoken for the one concrete situation and yet lets flow from itself the words which will illuminate every particular situation. This happens in its interpretation, which is a faithful and living repetition of what it says for the particular present moment. This is true not only of the apostolic words, but especially of the words of the Lord. The four Gospels themselves bear witness to this fact, for in them we have the words (and naturally also the deeds) of Jesus in the interpretation of the evangelists, which is often quite varied. But in each one of these developments the original word is present, according to the conviction of the evangelists and of the Church. This openness of the words of Scripture is, however, not only the objective reason for the necessity and justification of preaching on Scripture, but it is also the justification of a theology of the New Testament. It even demands beside, and after, "biblical theology" so called (which we characterized above according to the views of H. Schlier) a "dogmatic" view.

This "dogmatic" view no longer considers the contents of faith in the manner in which they present themselves in Scripture and in the religious reflexion in Scripture, "but seeks, within the area opened up and basically defined by the think-

71

ing of Scripture, to think its way beyond it to the object itself, in constant dialogue with the knowledge, experience, and decisions of the Church which are preserved in tradition." [25] That takes place, for example, in the ideas of the "justice of God," "justification," "sacrament," "transubstantiation," and so forth. It should not now call forth objections that such knowledge employs ideas and words which are foreign to the Bible. "By thinking its way towards the object itself the believing mind of the Church is not moving away from the contents of revelation, but is coming nearer to them. What was thought in the thinking in faith of Scripture and reflected on by biblical theology, was thought of by the latter before dogmatic theology comes to and thinks its way through it—and sometimes thinks it through to the end. The 'thinking through to the end,' which takes place in the consensus of faith in the Church, can, insofar as the whole and also the moment of the intellectual situation require and permit it, lead to a formulation in dogma. . . . Dogma does not mean the end of reflexion, but the raising of what has been thought into what is unquestionably and unloseably worthy of being remembered." [26]

The idea of dogma has had such a psychologically devastating effect right up to the present day chiefly because it has been seen only in the light of its being a more or less arbitrary decree by authority. Historical reminiscences like "inquisition," "persecution," "burning at the stake," and suggestive words such as "condemnation," "anathema," and so on create an atmosphere which in fact makes the word "dogma," in these circumstances, almost intolerable. Although we do not need to deny these phenomena, which must be understood in terms of the spirit and the language of their time, they are still not finally decisive for the true meaning of dogma. Our earlier

[25] *Ibid.*, p. 31.
[26] *Ibid.*, pp. 31-32.

investigation into the history of the word showed not only that it was taken into the language of theology and the Church relatively late, so that it was, and is, exchangeable, but it has shown that the imposition on such a meaning is historically and systematically untrue to the total situation even if the theology of the past is not without responsibility for this misunderstanding.

6. THE LIVING WORD OF THE GOSPEL AS THE PRIMARY FORM OF TRADITION AND ITS RELATION TO THE DOGMA OF THE CHURCH

We shall endeavor to clarify this confusion in respect of this authoritative element by showing in the following section how the hidden inner unity of Scripture, which points dynamically beyond itself, is preserved concretely and made present in the process of the interpretation of the revelation history that Scripture incorporates.

Such an investigation must start by unmasking the *false* appearance of writing fixed for all time which Scripture generally and perhaps even in the preceding discussion suggests. We must again realize more clearly its quality as occasional writing. The Gospels can never deny their origin in the bosom of the living Church, as is confirmed by modern research into the history of form and compilation, that is, of tradition. It is difficult to imagine how much the revealing events of Good Friday, Easter, and Pentecost meant for the knowledge in faith of the pre-Easter Jesus. The previous history of Jesus acquires through them a new meaning and actuality for the foundation of the belief in the Messiah and also for the concrete way of life of those who believed in Christ. "Going back to the earthly life of Jesus necessarily involved the making

73

present and using of his pre-Easter history and preaching, in relation to the quite different situation of the Church which had come into being after Easter and Pentecost. The history of Jesus after Easter was therefore *from the beginning up to the time that it was formulated in writing* in the earlier gospels *a living tradition*, which was stamped not only by the profounder insights given into the revelation of Christ by Good Friday and the events of Easter, but also by the questions and the needs of the early Church. That is, *the handing on of the contents of the history of Jesus was already in its pre-literary stage a tradition which was related to the needs of the actual time*" [27] (italics added).

This state of affairs also indicates that the primary mode of the presence of the word of the Gospel was the personal presence of the witness and the preacher. With all his freedom to engage in genuine thinking about his faith the witness is in no way autonomous. As a faithful *witness* he can vouch for the purity of the word. The word is not only relatively independent and effective by itself, but also master over the apostle (see especially with Paul in the Second Epistle to the Corinthians). But that does not mean that the word acquires complete independence and becomes an hypostasis or a quasi-hypostatic entity. The Gospel is primarily that which is heard, that which is passed on to be heard and thus is truly obedience.[28] The presence of the word is decisive for its being heard. This basic situation creates that tension, which cannot be removed, between the task of preserving and that of making present. No

[27] A. Vögtle, "Werden und Wesen der Evangelien," in *Diskussion über die Bibel* (Mainz², 1964), pp. 56-57; see pp. 47-84.
[28] There is a play on words here, unreproducible in English. "*Gehorsam*," "obedience," comes from the same root as "*hören*," "to hear (and obey)."—Tr.

foreign elements may be added—and yet the message must at all times be proclaimed and interpreted, made clear to men. In spite of the great variety of the kerygma the various evangelists still feel themselves committed to a common confession of faith (see Ephesians 4, 5-6 alone). It is difficult to discern directly a material unity, and it is true that in the New Testament there are certainly statements which are like formulas, and that there is no one particular formula which is used in an identical form by all the early Christian witnesses to the kerygma of what has been revealed in Jesus Christ. However, it is still undeniable that the "word" of the death and resurrection of the Lord had been already shaped *before* the New Testament writings into formula-type statements and, in the form of a real tradition of the faith of early Christianity, had influenced the emerging writings in diverse ways (as liturgical, hymnic material, or as catechetical, parenetic material, and so forth). Nevertheless, one can discern in these various traditions a few original forms in which the essential theological ideas are expressed. "In fact, the history of the New Testament tradition has shown ever more clearly that the New Testament writings embrace a number of fixed traditions of faith and especially of credal formulas which both consciously and unconsciously influence them and their kerygma. For example, a fixed paradosis had a decisive influence on the formation of the account of the passion and the theology behind it. Schemata of the original proclamation of faith and of original credal formulas emerge repeatedly and at important places in Acts and in the Epistles, appearing as norms of faith which are then developed in the text. . . . One is nevertheless able to observe certain theological principles underlying the theology of the New Testament writings, which are committed to and develop them. Thus it is clear that the theology which is found in the New Testament writings implies the prior existence of concrete apostolic parathesis as the immediate source of belief." [29]

Perhaps the importance of these traditions of belief has been seen in a false perspective. There is no straight line into the developed confessions of faith of the early Church, as if these were the direct final result of New Testament theology and the now finally fixed document of Church unity. ". . . we must keep in mind that the credal formulas of the original Church come *before* the New Testament, and that those of the early Church do not proceed solely from it. The historical process was probably that written and oral tradition were formulated and fixed in the symbols and that the embodiment of the apostolic heritage in Scripture and in the symbols were each separate events which nevertheless influenced each other." [30] Thus the tradition and the shaping of the gospels in relation to the essential statements about the death and resurrection of the Lord had already taken place in the pre-literary stage, statements which had been gathered in the credal traditions, as if in a center of crystallization, and which the rest of the tradition followed. "There was never any tradition which did not always have its place in the life of the believing community." [31] Such knowledge must have deeper theological consequences. First of all, it shatters the superficial idea of "Scripture" as a clear and incontestable, fixed and unambiguous result which does not require that one investigate the constitutive elements

[29] Schlier, *op. cit.*, pp. 15-16. See also *ibid.*, note 20 containing references to the works of R. Bultmann, M. Dibelius, W. Hillmann, K. H. Schelkle, J. R. Geiselmann. See also G. Schille, "Das Leiden des Herrn," in *Zeitschrift für Theologie und Kirche* 52 (Tübingen, 1955), pp. 161-205.

[30] Schlier, *op cit.*, p. 20, note 25.

[31] G. Bornkamm, "Geschichte und Glaube im NT," in *Evangelische Theologie* 22 (Munich, 1962), p. 13.

of its pre-history and make use of these in their factual significance. These insights of form history are almost common-
places, but theology, and especially the account of such things
as "dogma," tends to undervalue their theological worth. This
oral tradition was particularly exposed to the dangers of its
own history. It could become distorted in every way, essential
portions could be forgotten, and inappropriate extensions
added; or it could become involved with dangerous Gnostic
or other Hellenistic myths; or it could be made into an extract,
in the manner of a moral code. "But the remarkable thing is
that, against this danger which the historical character of the
tradition presented, the claim of the revelation event maintained itself, though often threatened, but ultimately safe-
guarded, in its language and its interpretation, which were the
language and the interpretation of the early Church, in the
power of the Spirit, through and for Scripture. For Scripture
states, preserves, and perfects the tradition in the way that the
subject matter itself demands. It is also gathered into the
Church like a harvest. The word of the revelation event
manifests itself fully in, and for, time in Scripture. In Scripture it inscribes itself in history for history. In Scripture it
finds its final form in the world of the provisional and thus
fulfills its intentions. For the event of revelation desires to be
present everywhere at all times. It was an event in the sense
that, although in itself it was directed towards the immediate
world around it, it tended towards a boundless horizon of experience. But through Scripture it becomes related to everything." [32] When the canon had been finally decided, this act
was to be understood only as one of the Church's confessions
of faith. In practical terms, that means that before there was a
"canon" and hence also, before what we call "Scripture," in

---

[32] Schlier, *op. cit.*, pp. 46-47.

the full sense, the Church had already created another criterion. A. von Harnack formulates the fact of this pre-
eminence of an original *regula fidei* in drastic terms: "The
canon was originally the rule of faith; Scripture has, in fact,
come between it and us." [33]

This living rule of faith (see 1 Clement 7, 2: canon of paradosis) is to be dated not later than the establishment of "Scripture." "The existence of New Testament writings which are
acknowledged as apostolic does not necessarily include the
existence of a 'New Testament' as 'Scripture'—it is a long path
from the writings to Scripture. It is a well-known fact, and
one to be taken account of, that the New Testament nowhere
describes itself as 'Scripture'; for it, only the Old Testament is
'Scripture,' while the message of Christ is the 'spirit' which
teaches one to understand that Scripture. The idea of a 'New
Testament' as 'Scripture' is still quite unimaginable—even in
those places where the idea of 'Church office' acquires a clear
shape as the form of paradosis. This open situation of the existence of recognized New Testament writings without there
being a principle of Scripture or a clear conception of a canon
of the New Testament lasts until well into the second century
—until the middle of the period of the conflict with
Gnosticism." [34]

With reference to the words of St. Augustine that the
regula fidei was "*de scripturarum planioribus locis et ecclesiae
auctoritate*" *(De Doct. Christ.,* III, 2, 2), J. Ratzinger has
pointed out that here "*scripture sui insius interpres*" is, in a
sense, affirmed, inasmuch as the *regula* which makes the meaning of Scripture clear is itself taken from Scripture; but there
is then something beyond Scripture, because the authority of

---

[33] *Dogmengeschichte* II (Tübingen², 1910) p. 87, note 3.

[34] J. Ratzinger and K. Rahner, *Episkopat und Primat* (Freiburg², 1963),
p. 47; ET *Episcopacy and Primacy* (New York, 1962).

the Church fixes the "canon" as the expression of its faith. The *regula fidei*, which is also called *"fides"* until the late Middle Ages and is identical with the later idea of dogma, is primarily not an aggregate of propositions but a "rule" in the sense of a primary "principle" of faith, namely, of the living faith of the Church itself, by means of which the latter binds itself to divine revelation. The *regula fidei*, seen in this light, is not merely *fides quae*, but also *fides qua*. [35]

One cannot counter this view with the objection that this argument makes the Church the mistress over the Scriptures. The relations between the two are more complicated than that. The apostolic succession and emphasis on the "word" of the "Gospel" are not antithetical. The succession is accepting the service of the word, it is testimony to the message that has been entrusted to it. "The office, the succession of the apostles, is based on the word. . . . Succession means holding fast to the apostolic word, as tradition means the continued existence of authorized witnesses." [36]

Protestant theology sees the word rather as an independent corrective of the Church's own power. "In its opinion God's word can break such a commitment," a "commitment" of the word of God to an episcopal succession.[37] This question cannot be further pursued here, but it must be pointed out that the idea for the apostolic succession did not arise from a merely external principle in order to legitimate the handing on of the kerygma; rather it grew out of the highly interconnected unity of word, sacrament, mission, and service. The word cannot exist without the office, although the witness is

[35] Thus above all Ratzinger, "Tradition III (systematisch)," in *Lexikon für Theologie und Kirche* X (1965).
[36] J. Ratzinger and K. Rahner, *Episcopat und Primat*, p. 46.
[37] See K. E. Skydsgaard, "Kirche IV," *Lexikon für Theologie und Kirche* VI (1961), p. 185.

tied to the word and remains committed to it. He is, after all, only a witness *inasmuch* as he feels himself bound by it. The rank and authority of the word are indeed to be defended against many tendencies within Catholic theology and many Catholic practices. Moreover, Church office is by no means dependent on the attitude of the person who holds it. It is not possible here to go into the relation between the office, properly understood as a service of reconciliation and of the word, with Church unity. We have sought only to make clear the reciprocal character of the bond between the witness and the word, and the word and the witness, so that it might appear why these inter-connections between Scripture and tradition are possible and necessary, why the canonicity of "Scripture" is given through the faith of the Church, and why the genuine antithesis of Church and Scripture on the basis of a most intimate bond between them involves a mutual interpenetration which justifies fully the serious claims that Scripture has on the Church.

This discussion was intended primarily to demonstrate the fact that the "matter" of the "gospel" and the authority of the word which is manifested in Church doctrine are not two separate entities which are afterwards brought together in a further operation. Of course, there are many important things that have not been mentioned: the presence of the Spirit in the Church; the correct idea of "infallibility," which assigns appropriate importance to the infallibility of the total Church *in credendo*, and which would make clear the charismatic basis of infallibility, so often overlooked, as opposed to its juridical aspects; the proper function of the teaching office as the norm of faith (which in this very quality is something other than the significance of Scripture as the norm of faith); the proper understanding of "tradition"; and many other matters which require fuller discussion.

However, on such a controversial theological point it is not possible to manage with arguments alone. The "dogmatic" cannot be separated from the conception of obedience and listening within the events of revelation. Moreover, in spite of all the labor of dogmatic "thinking," Christian faith remains at this point because it is *Christian* dogmatic thinking the "folly of the cross," which knows that it cannot demonstrate and clarify everything, since the pilgrim within the Church as it moves on its way does not see the truth, but believes it.

Thus a penetrating analysis of Christian "faith"—of the supernatural nature of faith, the freedom of faith, the darkness of faith, the special "eyes of faith," and so forth—would grant a deeper insight into the dogmatic. The central stumbling block is the idea of the "infallibility" of the Church's teaching office. No conciliatory avoidance of this issue is of value in the present situation of the ecumenical dialogue. Hard fronts at least have contours. Let us quote von Harnack: "With the death of the old idea of 'Church' the old idea of 'dogma' and hence 'dogma' itself are also done away with; for a dogma without infallibility does not mean anything. Its death-knell was sounded by Luther in his attitude at the Leipzig disputation, although he himself never fully recognized the full implications of what he said, nor the unsatisfactory nature of his contradictory substitute for it, a semi-biblicism. He is splendid when he takes his stand on his living faith; but the objective gap it creates remains unfilled and unfillable. Hence in the first edition of my *History of Dogma* I noted the 'end' of dogma in the sixteenth century." [38]

Such an uncompromising position should not blind one to the importance of the questions that it raises. "Where is the

[36] "Briefwechsel mit Adolf von Harnack und ein Epilog," in E. Peterson, *Theologische Traktate* (Munich, 1951), p. 303 (Letter of 7. 7. 1928); see pp. 293-321.

constitutive element of the Christian faith, that which is actually to be passed on, the *traditio tradenda*, if on the one hand it is kerygma, word, and Gospel, and on the other hand the Holy Spirit and not the letter—although never the Holy Spirit without the letter? What is the one that appears as variable? What is so-called kerygma, if not only illegitimate but also legitimate changes could be made in it?" [39]

In order to demonstrate even more clearly the nature of dogma and its limitations, let us attempt in conclusion to describe briefly the basic features of a dogmatic statement.

B. *The Basic Elements of a Dogmatic Statement*

A dogmatic statement is characterized by the following features, although we do not claim our list to be exhaustive.

(1) First of all, a dogmatic statement claims to be true in that formal sense which we are familiar with from ordinary everyday language. The dogmatic statement fulfills all the inner structures and laws that a non-religious statement does, or may do: the relation to the person making the statement, the historical nature of the conceptual elements, the involvement in a historical and sociological context, a logical structure, a variety of literary forms and types, unknown and unconsciously shared areas and affinities of experience between the speaker and the listener without which there could be no real possibility of understanding and agreement. These and similar structures of a natural statement must also be found in the dogmatic statement. It is the task of dogmatics, as a branch of knowledge, to follow up these hermeneutic conditions and to present them in the context of their factual and historical

[39] Ebeling, *Wort Gottes und Tradition,* pp. 153-154.

involvement. We still lack today a comprehensive logic of the dogmatic statement. Such an undertaking requires first of all a great deal of philosophical investigation of matters that are by no means obvious (see, for example, the meaning and the structure of a word, of a statement, a proposition, language as a hermeneutic medium altogether, the relation of the natural language of everyday to "terminology," the need for and the laws of a history of ideas, and so forth).

A further, not unimportant aspect of a dogmatic statement, inasmuch as it is a true statement, may be briefly noted: it is *true*, because a human statement bears within itself this meaning and this claim. It refers to a specific state of affairs which exists independently of the speaker (or at any rate is not simply identical with him); it is not merely an articulating statement of a subjective state in the speaker. It does not seek to give an objective form to the subjectivity of the speaker but to impress on the listener the apparent state of affairs in itself, and hence the reality that is meant. That such a statement may contain subjective elements, in a still unspecified sense, is simply part of the nature of such a statement. But the value of a dogmatic statement must not be determined by these elements alone. It is necessary to emphasize this primary objective meaning because, following in the wake of some basic tendencies of modern philosophy, themselves already reduced in a primitive fashion to a common denominator, the significance and value of a dogma are measured only according as it is the *immediate* expression of a living experience which is actually present or clearly remembered. If this aspect does play a part in the properly understood idea of dogma, the basic description of it should not be exclusively oriented towards its adequacy in this respect. This is not to deny that a dogmatic statement may in certain circumstances appear in a conceptual framework and in an area of interpretation which does not translate adequately

83

every side of the phenomenon originally envisaged. No doubt, there are transformations which communicate the original phenomena in concepts, modes of thought, and a range of understanding which do not perhaps makes clear the innermost individuality of what has been heard and which have an alienating effect because they take over certain presuppositions (for example, the adoption of a particular ontology, of the world-understanding appropriate to it, of a language which is stamped by a different world-understanding that exercises an implicit, hidden influence on it, and so forth). But if one raises this possibility, which in view of human finitude is always partially fulfilled, to an absolute principle, then one must see all language and statement which appear "foreign" to us today as a misunderstanding and an objective fixing of meaning which obscures more than it reveals. Thus, for example, the Christology and Trinitarian doctrine of the older Church have become suspect, without any attempt being made to recover the perspective in which they might still contribute something essential, even if what we see proves to be for us today just one aspect among many, so that its historical limitations become apparent.

We do not do the historical facts justice if, for example, from the point of view of a superficial and inadequately founded ontology of existence we regard the ontological foundations of the great dogmatic statements of the older Church as naïve speculation which is oriented only towards the reality of things and the related ontology of *"Vorhandenheit."* [40] H. Jonas gives a very good example of this misunderstanding when he says that dogma presents an undialectical object proposition, which he interprets in the following way:

---

[40] An untranslateable existential term which expresses the physical presence of things in an objectively conceived world of time and space. —Tr.

III. FROM KERYGMA TO DOGMA

"The 'objects,' visible quantities and events, set against a unified objective horizon of reality, possess a representative character symbolical of the original, inner-existential phenomena, which thus make contact with us through them in the mode of facts and processes analogous to things."[41] The fundamental act which makes this objectification, in the modern sense, possible, is ultimately a "fundamental self-objectification" and the ontological transformation of what is originally existentially given into a so-called "word-conceptuality." Jonas can therefore logically go on to say, "Hence ultimately all dogmas are self-objectifications." Thus the interpretation of dogmas has meaning only if, by a specifically "dialectic" method, it breaks through and cancels out the apophantic, objective "fixing" in words. Although such an interpretation remains basically correct when it sees in this classical theology the noticeable effect of an ontology which is primarily oriented to "nature," the generalization of such a thesis is false if in the narrow perspective of a particular conception within modern philosophy it limits this view to that of a view of the world which take mere "objects" as its measure. This would be to make of a "unified objective horizon of reality" a formalized "objectivity" which has almost nothing to do with the much richer idea of "nature" and of the "thing" in a mode of thought influenced by Greek and medieval models.

Closely connected with this misunderstanding is another: that whereas in the view we have just outlined dogma has only a "representative symbolic character," that is, does not itself actually state the object, the not merely inner-existential phenomena referred to, a true dogmatic statement knows that

---

[41] *Augustin und das Paulinische Freiheitsproblem* (Göttingen, 1930), pp. 67f.; see pp. 66-76.

it does not refer to objects of immediate sense experience and does not simply offer its own spiritual experience, that is, it knows that what it says can be only an analogy. It refers to the intended state of affairs with the aid of positive modes of statement and their intensification by transcendence and negativity, but in the awareness that this transcendental surpassing of what was originally given does not lead first to the obscure and the nameless. Because a dogmatic statement in this sense desires to be a question of truth, not all dogmatic statements can be equally true and false. The modern attempt to regard such a statement as true if it succeeds in adequately embodying subjective, existential, and unique religious experience, that is, making it productive within and without, is thwarted by this demand of the statement itself for the validity of what it states. This is not to deny that there is a difference between the truth which is revealed through a pre-conceptual, pre-propositional insight and in a direct personal way, and that truth (or error) given in the objective conceptual statement of that truth which is unobjective, pre-conceptual, and involved in a multiplicity of implications. This pre-conceptual insight can be true even though its conceptual expression is false (and vice versa). This pre-propositional insight, however, is always an insight into the state of affairs in question, which has its visible existence in itself and is to be differentiated within the situation of being known, although it is not accessible without the latter.

(2) If a dogmatic statement has the characteristics of an otherwise "natural" statement, then being "natural" does not mean that the statement is made within the abstract area of "pure nature." If statements in general already contain a tension between what is meant and what is said, then this potential divergence is seen to the full in the theological state-

meaning of an objectified statement, he may seem to profess ment. Thus, for example, it is possible for someone to believe truly in Christ although, judged according to the objective only unbelief. Or again, no one can know of himself or of someone else automatically and with perfect certainty whether he truly believes, although he may appear (according to public testimony and also according to the profoundest witness of one's own reflexion) to hold firmly to the statement or faith, declared to be absolute truth. These facts are unintelligible unless one realizes that a dogmatic statement is formulated and created by man, who stands with his concrete nature within a fallen order. The darkening of the human mind caused by original sin and the (partly related) moral need of revelation for the clear and certain knowledge of those truths which are of themselves available to the natural knowledge of man in the religious and moral field—this influence of human sinfulness should not simply be related to the moral field or used to characterize the knowledge of man outside revelation. At least in broad outline it is possible to maintain that even human knowledge and statements within the area of revelation and of the faith of the Church betray the shadows and the scars of that wound; according to Catholic teaching even the justi-fied man is still partly affected by his sinful origin. Granted that we do not regard the *formal* differentiation between true and false statements as the ultimate achievement of mortal knowledge and imagine that a statement which is valid in the abstract is removed for all time from the region of sin and the flesh, we will have to admit that a dogmatic state-ment and the intellectual efforts which converge in it also bear the stamp of guilt and sin. At any rate, we shall certainly have to consider whether a statement which in itself must be described as true cannot also be over-hasty, presumptuous, and offensive, whether it does not also betray an unkind

tendency in sinful man to "dogmatize" (at least in a manner
that is often condescending, which suggests the enjoyment
of a harsh formulation). Cannot a truth also be dangerous,
ambiguous, and tempting, when stated in an impertinent and
over-clever way, so that it forces the other man into a situation
of decision which is in a certain measure inappropriate to him?
Is it permissible to claim so automatically that historically
determined perspectives are the epitome of all truth so that
the representatives of this incontestable truth appear, to the
irritation of those with whom they are engaged in dialogue,
as the *beati possidentes?* Even if there is no definitive and
unambiguous answer to this problem, these questions must still
be asked, because they do not contradict the basic data of
Catholic theology.

(3) Even if one distinguishes the dogmatic statement from
the kerygmatic, it still remains in its essence a statement of
faith. It is such not merely in what it says *about* a theological
situation, but also in the very fact that it is made at all, that
is, as a *fides qua creditur*. Traditional theology has expressed
this truth partly by presenting the act of theology as a *habitus
scientiae* which is, however, filled and supported by the *habitus
fidei* (see also the "*fide illustrata*": Denzinger 3016). Because
the inner debate of the listener with what is said to him is
an essential element in listening, a certain degree of theology
belongs to listening. Pure listening in faith is an activity which
already involves individual modes of thinking, experiencing,
and speaking. A first basic "theological" reflexion takes place
in the merely obedient listening to the word of God. That
means, however, that dogmatic reflexion and its statement can
and must never be completely separated from its own origin:
from faith itself in its character as an act.

This view is by no means automatic for a large part of post-

Tridentine school theology. If one considers grace, inasmuch as it is strictly supernatural, as something that is absolutely beyond consciousness, that is, if one denies that the supernatural saving acts have a formal object which cannot be grasped by any natural act, then the object of theology and of the dogmatic statement can be grasped equally well by purely natural reason as by believing reason. The unbeliever grasps just the same truths as the believer. Against this view, which pushes the nature of faith into a dimension which is conceived as purely objectivistic, circumstantial, and outside the spiritual act as such, one can, with good reason and with the support of a growing number of theologians (especially of our century), hold to the Thomist doctrine of the special formal object of the act performed in grace and of the consequent incommensurability of faith with a profane act (even if the latter refers to religious matters). From within this position one may say (and especially of pure listening) that a dogmatic statement and the reflexion involved in it is an act of faith.

The profane student of religion does not automatically see a dogmatic statement in the same way as a theologian does. The insight which is conveyed in it is determined before its actual articulation in the statement by the act of the person who accepts or rejects grace. The unbeliever, who is by no means automatically the man without grace, stands under grace in the mode of closing himself to it, even if he refuses to see what he does see and "suppresses" the truth. Here also no one can say which of the speakers belongs concretely and absolutely to one or the other category. This also makes clear why the dogmatic statement shares in the confessing and praising statement of the heard and obediently accepted Gospel of Jesus Christ (see, therefore, the correct meaning of the doxological element in dogma). That is why in spite of all reflexion, the dogmatic statement goes straight to the historical saving event and presents it. It not only speaks "about" this event, it is not merely concerned with a "proposition," but is *ex fide ad fidem*. The theological description of the act of faith will have to become separated far more from its involvement with a wrongly understood understanding of dogmatic statement, in order to be able truly to show how faith "thinks" as faith.

(4) A dogmatic statement is a statement that is in a special measure a statement by the *Church*. This idea has already been treated (from various points of view) in the foregoing. Here we are able to emphasize one element only which has so far not been considered. Theology exists because the act of faith should take place within the Church, inspired by the Church, and in relation to the Church. Of course, there is also a theology of an "individual." But in such a socially tangible body as the Church the specifically dogmatic character of theological statements emerges more clearly. Theology is the continuance in history of a revelation which took place at a particular point in space and time, a revelation which constantly takes place again in a new encounter and assimilates to itself all men's experience of life. If the historical event were not given once and for all, there would be a constant revelation and never theology referring to a saving event limited by space and time, an event which is not identical with theology. If there were no theology, salvation history, which has taken place once and for all, would not be able to reach man in later ages in his world and offer him salvation. At any rate, he would not be reached in the full extent of his existence; he would have to strip off his historical uniqueness like a cloak and, as an abstract man-in-himself, seek to discover a relationship with this past saving event. Hence it is more easily under-

stood that theology has the bindingness of faith itself if it is to be the absolutely obedient confrontation of one's own existence by the kerygma of salvation in Jesus Christ, who appeared once and for all; and since it is the Church that it is believed in common, faith is confessed in common, and God is praised for his grace in a language that can be spoken by all, theology acquires an especially Church significance. In confrontation with a common spiritual situation, which must be ever anew understood and experienced in community *as* something in common, the inherited Gospel must be laid hold of ever anew in this community. Thus there must be theology in the Church, carried on by the Church itself, even if it acquires an important part of its life from the initiative of individuals. The question of the individual also is always directed to the Church, the question whether it can make a particular statement its own or at least tolerate it as something that is possible within the one Church. Apart from and above this theology of the individual, related as it is always to the Church, there is a theology of the Church, in which the Church pursues theology as a whole in its constituted teaching office through its representatives—that is, functioning within a particular historical situation it reflects on its religious awareness and its original source, the Gospel of and about Jesus Christ which has been handed down in the faith of the original Christian community. In the form of this new theological reflexion it proclaims anew the one constant faith in such a way that it retains and achieves again the strongest possible immediate confrontation and challenge for the man hearing it. This theology is also a real proclamation of faith which demands obedience inasmuch as the Church, in its teaching authority, can make the claim that its Gospel, thus constituted, that is, transformed into theology, *is* (and is not just *about*) the form, valid here and now, of the word in which

91

God has spoken to us. Thus is the theological point from which an essential definition of dogmatic statement must begin.

(5) Because a dogmatic statement has this Church significance, it also always involves a terminological ruling on community language, which may, on the one hand, be binding, and on the other must be taken account of in the interpretation of the Church's explanations and must not be confused with the object itself, or with a statement that is only possible because it is based on the object. The truth aimed at in theological statements is of boundless variety and infinite plenitude. The conceptual instruments available to describe this reality are quite finite. They remain finite also when they grow in the history of ideas and words. Since a theological statement must be appropriate to the believing consciousness of a fairly large sociological group, and therefore the finitude of the terminology must be even greater, the task of keeping open with this conceptual material, the awareness of the richly differentiated and comprehensive fullness of what faith is directed towards is enormously difficult. Such finite conceptual material can never be adequate to the object to be conveyed. Such words can only emphasize certain features of the situation to be described and inevitably neglect others, failing to draw sufficient attention to other signposts to essential truths of faith. Moreover, it is quite impossible to give always an absolutely unambiguous, spontaneous definition of the concepts used.

Hence the doctrinal pronouncements of the Church and theological statements imply a fixed terminology, which cannot be questioned according to its truth, but at most according to its suitability. This fixed nature of their terminology is not necessarily present to the minds of those teaching and defining, and perhaps is generally unconscious. It cannot be grasped adequately by reflecting human reason. On the edge of the history of dogma such insights appear even in official declarations, when for example the event of the Last Supper is to be interpreted and the Church calls this event *"aptissime"* (see Denzinger 1652 and 1642) transubstantiation. Pius XII, for example, defends in his encyclical *Humani generis* the appropriateness of many concepts which are rooted in the scholastic tradition. He says that it should not be assumed that the Church will abandon them, although it is known that they have become historical (see Denzinger 3881-3883).

This problem, however, is far more easily grasped in the practice of Church doctrine. If, say, it is taught that man is a sinner ever since the time of Adam, the word "sinner" is used here only in a very analogous sense (see, for example, the sin of the personal and private decision). There are even some examples which show that from time to time the Church has not only slightly shaded the terminology, but has actually (without changing anything in what is objectively referred to) changed the concepts it uses. Thus the concepts of St. Augustine in respect of the sinfulness of every act of man afflicted by original sin was once Church terminology, but these have been implicitly surrendered by the declarations of Pius V. Augustine was able, and had, to maintain—and the Church of his time did so as well in its doctrine—that every unjustified sinner sinned in every one of his acts. In the language of the post-Tridentine Church it is impossible to formulate things in this way, although it can be shown that the differing formulations do not, with regard to what they refer to, contradict one another. What Church Christology and Trinitarian doctrine call "person" has in fact little to do with what we are accustomed to call by this name. But here again one is not able within the area of Church doctrine to express the intended object in words that completely ignore this way of expressing it. A further example is better known: the question of who is a member of the Church is very much a ruling on the use of terminology. The conceptual differences that we see between, for example, the encyclical *Mystici corporis* and the recent decrees and constitutions of the Second Vatican Council are astonishing. From this one may be permitted to conclude that these declarations of the Church's teaching office never see the question explicitly as one of terminology, but impart doctrine in the understanding that it is the subject itself that is being talked about. This hidden pre-eminence of "nature" language and its effectiveness against all terminology would be a new phenomenon, the significance of which for a total evaluation of dogmatic statements would need to be more fully worked out with the aid of modern linguistic philosophy and hermeneutics. To mention only one important element: the vagueness that comes with this pre-eminence of "natural" language (see, for example, the concept *"substantia"* in "transubstantiation" which in the Tridentine definition is not meant in the way in which it is used in scholastic terminology; see also the importance of the idea of "form" for the understanding of the unity in man between the body and the soul, an idea which must not be interpreted in the strictly hylemorphistic sense) keeps the field open for various interpretations. A limit is set, certainly, in that such "formulations" are polemically directed against definite heterodox opinions. It is only this that gives such definitions their definite concrete quality and also their bindingness (see, for example, the fact that the definitions of the whole of sacramental theology at the Council of Trent, fundamentally, were merely directed against Protestant theology, as the researches of H. Lennerz and P. Fransen have recently shown). This is seen perfectly in such decisions as those of Chalcedon, where the words "unmixed and unseparated" were used consciously in order to draw limits within which the matter referred to is still by no means clear. There is even a mutual recognition of different dogmatic formulations as, for example, the whole argument about the *"filioque"* clause, in which traditions and modes of speaking that have grown up in different historical contexts are, under the appropriate conditions, mutually recognized.

It is, therefore, to be remembered that these ideas are inevitably subject to a constant historical change which is undoubtedly influenced by the authoritative teaching office of the Church—in part directed, held up, partly guided into other channels, as is permissible—but that this historical development of terminology cannot be wholly determined, even within the Church, by its teaching authority. Thus it takes place independently of the official Church and its conscious direction, at least in part, and this fact implies also the right, and perhaps in individual situations the duty, of the Church to take account of this process which is taking place independently of it.

Someone who is not immediately at home in this theology of the Church or who is involved too unquestioningly in its formulations without being aware of the historical qualification of such a problem fails equally to grasp the measure of doctrinal decisions which are strictly binding. The traditional method, division, and mode of arguing in dogmatics is not without responsibility for this situation. Not every well-attested consensus of faith within the whole Church must reach a dogmatically fixed conclusion or be "defined." Dogma grows at a much deeper level in the not easily plumbed depths of freedom and necessity in a situation which can only with difficulty be seen as a whole. G. Ebeling is, for example, undoubtedly wrong when in his essay "Zur Frage nach dem

Sinn des mariologischen Dogmas"[42] he sees the *"Assumpta"* definition as the dogmatization of the basic structure of Catholicism. It would need another lengthy investigation to show that the situation is much more open than that. The Second Vatican Council itself—in spite of all the limitations to which these decisions also are subject—has shown here, *even as a teaching authority of the Church,* an openness and a possibility of development which burst the bonds of these over-simple schemata.

Thus a Catholic theologian can remain tied to an officially adopted conceptuality even if he cannot, or need not, conceal from himself the problems of the "terminology" connected with it—with its ambiguities, perhaps even its lack of perspective (which is the important thing), and other such finite deficiences of any terminology as such. That is not to say that the theologian is passive in relation to this linguistic ruling of the Church on theological terminology. Wherever he pursues living theology by looking at the object itself he also contributes actively—perhaps almost unnoticeably—to that constant historical development in the terminology of Church language. The contrary, however, is also true: by using the Church's terminology in his statements, he is placing himself within the historical and sociological limitations of the particular contemporary religious consciousness, which—if they are accepted and tolerated—at the same time keep the individual open to the religious consciousness of the Church, as well as expecting of him that renunciation without which there can be in this world no unity of truth and love.

(6) A theological statement is a *statement into the mystery.* As a statement it directs the listener beyond itself and into the

[42] Reprinted in *Wort Gottes und Tradition,* pp. 175-182; see esp. pp. 181-182.

mystery of God, as it is in itself. This is true of the dogmatic statement because, as already shown, it can never entirely divest itself of its connection with the original kerygmatic statement of faith. However intense the theological reflexion might be and the consequently stronger relation back, the statement of faith, when properly made, retains always the factual insight that the subject matter it refers to is only correctly named if—in spite of all the effort that the human mind expends in order to make it accessible—it is understood as having already been given by God, in his taking hold of man. The dogmatic statement, like the kerygmatic, has one basic feature which is not, unlike secular categorical statements, identical with the conceptual contents which it presents. Whatever its own meaning the latter remains always just the medium of the experience of being referred to what is above itself and above anything that is nameable. This phenomenon is not only empty transcendence, not merely the horizon for the possibility of "objective" conceptuality, but it is the way in which man actually moves towards the gracious self-communication of God. The *idea* of transcendence and the *idea* of grace is not what is meant here, but the things themselves. Of course, these realities cannot be presented in dogmatic form in a simple "objective" way in themselves; it cannot be established whether they are fully involved by the statement. The theologian can only be told again and again that what goes into his statements which he constructs out of ideas is not the only thing that there must be in those statements. Certainly, we may draw conclusions as to the quality of someone's mind (at least in the totality of what is said and in the long view), if he merely says that he is concerned with the mystery, but in fact treats his ideas and his propositions as if they were the object itself, as if they were controlled by him like self-contained monads and were not merely the signs which speak most clearly where they silently point out to the believer the way—beyond themselves—to the unapproachable lights of God. It would require special treatment to show that analogy, properly understood, is the basic structure of Catholic theology and hence also of the dogmatic statement. The important thing here is the insight that theological discourse does not only speak of the mystery, but does it correctly only if it is also a kind of indication of how to come face to face with the mystery oneself. It would undoubtedly be a mistake to imagine that one "possesses" the object when all one has is the conceptual word about it. This word itself has a genuine mystagogic significance: it induces the experience, in grace, of the absolute mystery.

(7) The dogmatic statement is an *eschatological phenomenon*. It is this primarily because it is directed in a specific way to the final age that has already started with the revelation in Jesus Christ. But its message is nothing other than the meaning of this new and final era. In this respect it is simultaneously an anticipation of the *eschaton* and therefore contains a prophetic quality. But that also means that the dogmatic statement is always talking about something which will only appear at an unimaginable future time in its total glory and splendor. Thus the dogmatic statement can only show forth in a provisional way the final state of things. It is part of the sobriety of dogmatic discourse to remain critically aware of this dual eschatological significance in dogmatic statement. Thus the seriousness which is necessary when dealing with the subject of *salvation* is preserved, but also the provisional nature of all theological formulation can remain more critically present to the mind.

(8) The dogmatic statement is *not identical with the original*

word of revelation. The difference between the original proclamation of revelation and the original statement of faith, on
the one hand, and dogmatically thought-through propositions
on the other has already been several times pointed out. We
have the prototype of the former mode of statement in Scripture, even if here perhaps the difference between the earlier
event of revelation and the immediate testimony to it on the
one hand, and reflexion on it in Scripture on the other, is to
be once more made note of.

Let us now proceed to set out the difference between the
dogmatic and the scriptural statement. In doing this we must
keep our eye on the characteristic of dogmatic statements
which we observed earlier, namely, that they still endeavor
to look towards the religious consciousness of the Church
and know that in this they are dependent on the teaching
office of the Church, even if they are not always, and in
every case, statements of a binding pronouncement by the
teaching office. Vice versa, that means, however, that there
can be no *proclaimed* revelation except in the form of *believed*
revelation. In every believed revelation there is, nevertheless,
as we have said, an element of reflexion in the hearer, and
hence an almost indissoluble unity and synthesis between
the word of God and the word of the particular man that he
alone, in his historical situation, can and must speak. The difference between the original kerygma and the dogmatic statement, therefore, does not consist in the fact that in the former
it is, as it were, the pure word of God that is given, and in
the latter only human reflexion on it. If this were the case
there could be only uncommitted theological discourse around
this word of God, but not a statement of belief which is different from it and yet absolutely binding, a statement of belief
to which the word of God (as it has originally been given to
men) retains its truly binding presence throughout the course

99

of history. There can be only a history of theology, but never a history of dogma.

It is essential to understand that even the simplest kerygmatic utterance contains an element of reflexion. Thus one scriptural statement may be secondary to another, from which it is derived. One cannot treat every passage as if it were on the same level of meaning and as if it were something which was wholly original, springing directly from the most immediate revelation of God (see the results of exegesis, in which not merely the *genus litterarium* of the "midrash" shows such a mode of procedure, but where the "anthology method," the *"relecture biblique,"* the "transposition of motifs," show the extent of this procedure).

The essential difference between theological statement (even in its binding form of an actual testimony of faith) and the original testimony of faith (to which *quoad nos* Scripture belongs as a whole) lies in the special unique position of Scripture. Revelation has a history: there are also quite specific events fixed in space and time by means of which this revelation, which is intended for all later ages, takes place in such a way that these later ages remain forever bound by it. The constant and unchanging *norma normans, non normata* for all later dogmatic statements reside in these events and the statements belonging to them which belong to the constitutive elements of the events themselves. These are the original statements, which in this quite specific sense are more than theology—even more than absolutely binding theology. They are the constant ground of all other future statements, they are what is handed down, not the developing tradition of what is handed down. There is no need to continue to discuss here the form in which this original statement of faith is given to us *norma normans, non normata* (both the statement of faith that demands the assent of faith and that which is not bind-

ing). Beyond the controversies concerning the place of tradition (see Chapter III, section 3), one can say that this norm
is given to us in Scripture. Even a source of tradition *apart*
from Scripture which would give us a testimony to the material contents of faith would not in fact be such that in it the
testimony, guaranteed as pure by God, of the actual, revealed,
apostolic tradition would be unalloyed with human tradition.

A more difficult question is *how* the Church can undertake
this necessary distinction between the human and the divine
in tradition which is always necessary if it is to know ever
anew the truth of a revelation and yet know that it is bound
to the original revelation. Nevertheless, Christians agree that
in Scripture the pure (even if completely historical) written
objectification of the apostolic kerygma is given to the Church,
in whatever way the former is determined, in more concrete
terms. Inasmuch as Scripture is this objective norm it remains
as an original word of revelation and faith in the Church and
of the Church, essentially different from every later theological statement of, and in, the Church, even if this moral
is a kerygmatic testimony of faith, a demand of faith, and not
only theological reflexion. Thus one could say that the theological word is a theological word alone only inasmuch as it
is not a scriptural one.

Here the whole scale of fluid transitions between theological
statements, in this strict sense, would have to be differentiated
(from the ordinary and extraordinary doctrinal pronouncement down to the private statement of an individual theologian). It may be doubted whether there is a true theology
of deduction which can achieve new insights and declare them
as not part of the contents of faith and hence not binding.
The main theological function of the theologically free dogmatic statement is certainly the better seeing, understanding,
and confessing of what is truly believed.

101

Hitherto we have considered more the difference between an original statement of faith and a theological and dogmatic statement that is dependent on it and grounded in it. There is also the difference between the statement which is confessional, referring to an object, trusting and praising what it contains, and the statement in which the first ray of thought is directed towards one's knowledge, even within this derived theological and dogmatic statement itself. This difference has its ultimate ontological ground in the nature of human knowledge, inasmuch as the latter is always both immediate and reflexive, in relation to itself and in relation to other things. This dualism cannot be fully overcome. That is why there is a dogmatic statement which is primarily concerned with the reflexive self-possession of knowledge about an object, and a dogmatic statement which is concerned with the object itself. With all their difference, the two kinds of statement can never be completely separated from each other.

In our earlier discussion of the history of the concept of "dogma" and related ideas we noted that at the close of the age of the Fathers "dogma" meant almost the same as what we today call "*depositum fidei*." This correspondence of the two ideas, however, has not persisted through the course of the history of dogma. So we must once again, this time more from a systematic viewpoint, consider to some extent the change in the meanings of these ideas.

The first reason for this differentiation is probably that the *depositum fidei*, as the basic essence of revelation, is not simply to be identified with fixed formulations and objectivized statements. There is by no means a settled situation of immutable propositions that could at any time be totally grasped and whose substance could be easily translated into any language one chooses inasmuch as another interpretation would appear at all necessary. The *depositum* is—to put it crudely—not something like a "bag of truth" of which the Church is custodian. But that does not mean that one vaporizes the essence of this heritage of faith into a number of indescribable experiences or feelings of a religious nature. The pure *depositum fidei* cannot be distilled out simply because it always appears in words and ideas which are conditioned by a particular pre-understanding of language, culture, and philosophy. One cannot simply abstract, methodically draw a line through, or put brackets around, everything that has been expressed in this way, linguistically and conceptually, in these statements. We saw that the "Gospel," in its pure essence as a direct, primary event of revelation in "Scripture," does not exist. Here also ultimate truth and the all-embracing mystery have not simply passed into the words or the written collection of gospels, epistles, and so forth which we have today. The *depositum fidei* also bears, obviously, the marks and qualities of that "Gospel" behind the "gospels" of which we spoke earlier. But how are we to conceive of such a *depositum* and the mode of its presence if it is not simply identical with the revelation of the New Testament? Does not this *depositum* refer back to *that*, or even *is* that of which the New Testament speaks? If the New Testament were simply "what has been set down in writing," then the *depositum fidei* could be only a duplication of Scripture in a, so to speak, more authentic form.

But the identification with the New Testament is undoubtedly too little. Nor is the *depositum fidei* a kerygmatic and theological first formula which would constitute the beginning of revelation. Exegetically, this "beginning" seems to have been quite varied even to the writers of the New Testament themselves. Thus the *depositum fidei* cannot be primarily only a "communication" of facts which have been stated once and for all. H. R. Schlette is undoubtedly correct when he emphasizes the *event* quality of the *depositum fidei*. Now this word "event" has such a varied meaning in contemporary philosophy and theology, or else arouses a number of similar conceptions which come, however, from quite varied pre-understandings, that one must make such a statement more concrete (see, for example, "event," in Barth, Heidegger, Fuchs, Ebeling, and their various schools). The event quality itself must not appear only in the "linguistic" event (Fuchs) or in the "event of the word" (Ebeling), for the salvation event goes back inescapably to historical acts. These are certainly accessible to us in the word, but the witness, the witness of authority, of the sacramental, and so forth, must not be lacking. Nor must the problem of the transmission of that original event be thrust aside, otherwise the "linguistic" event remains either abstract and isolated by itself, which means that one then circumvents Kierkegaard's inquiry after "contemporaneity" with Jesus Christ or else assumes an immediacy (which can never be *completely* denied) which spurns any historical understanding. Or else one no longer sees the true connection of this event with Jesus Christ (see, for example, 1 John 1, 1 ff.). This even reminds one strangely of Gnostic and purely speculative "ideas," even if one imagines that one has left all "metaphysics" far behind. Thus the event is a happening which is past and can only be experienced in the mode of the faith given by God, that is, simultaneously, in the Church. Because the concern is always to preserve the correct meaning of that original basic event and to interpret it in the best possible way in preaching and in common instruction throughout a long history, the *depositum fidei* can never be separated, in its event quality, from the language which belongs to it, a language which does not hesitate to embrace philosophical ideas of a bygone age, if only they can serve the one goal: to pronounce the essence of the constant origin of faith clearly within the dialogue of history. Perhaps the only way to counter irritation at the pre-eminence of "formulations," "theses," "anathematizations," and so forth is to follow these back to their original nature as words that can, and must, be spoken differently in a different historical situation. On this basis one could work out, for example, a typology of various modes of statement within the whole range of the "dogmatic" (compare, for example, a confession of faith with anathematizations and *canones*, and the unique quality of the statements at the Second Vatican Council).

That dogmatic statements are conditioned by the language of man and by his understanding of the world as revealed by language makes the question of what is constant in dogma more acute. These problems will have to be treated separately under the headings of "The Development of Dogma" and "The History of Dogma." The variety of the forms of Church statements must not, however, be limited solely to the dogmatic. The multiplicity of the kerygma in the New Testament is itself a testimony to the many ways in which the message of God has come to men and can still come to them today. Faith "thinks" in different ways, in poetry, in art, in music, and in the various practices of the Church. The liturgy has already been considered. These ways of transmitting the original kerygma can even help to combat the possible dangers of one-sided "dogmatizing" and offer new means for a deeper understanding of what is meant in fact by that idea which has become so ambiguous: "dogma."